Revolutionary Economies

Revolutionary Economies

What Archaeology Reveals about the Birth of American Capitalism

THOMAS W. CUDDY

A Division of
ROWMAN & LITTLEFIELD PUBLISHERS, INC.
Lanham • New York • Toronto • Plymouth, UK

ALTAMIRA PRESS
A division of Rowman & Littlefield Publishers, Inc.
A wholly owned subsidary of The Rowman & Littlefield Publishing Group, Inc.
4501 Forbes Boulevard, Suite 200
Lanham, MD 20706
www.altamirapress.com

Estover Road
Plymouth PL6 7PY
United Kingdom

British Library Cataloguing in Publication Information Available

Library of Congress Cataloguing-in-Publication Data

Cuddy, Thomas W., 1968–
  Revolutionary economies : what archaeology reveals about the birth of American
capitalism / Thomas W. Cuddy.
    p. cm.
  Includes index.
  ISBN-13: 978-0-7591-1178-3 (cloth : alk. paper)
  ISBN-10: 0-7591-1178-2 (cloth : alk. paper)
  ISBN-13: 978-0-7591-1179-0 (pbk. : alk. paper)
  ISBN-10: 0-7591-1179-0 (pbk. : alk. paper)
  eISBN-13: 978-0-7591-1229-2
  eISBN-10: 0-7591-1229-0
  1. Social archaeology—Chesapeake Bay Region (Md. and Va.) 2. Urban archaeology—
Chesapeake Bay Region (Md. and Va.) 3. Bakeries—Maryland—Annapolis—History—
18th century. 4. Bakeries—Virginia—Alexandria—History—18th century.
5. Capitalism—Social aspects—Maryland—Annapolis—History—18th century.
6. Capitalism—Social aspects—Virginia—Alexandria—History—18th century.
7. Annapolis (Md.)—Economic conditions—18th century. 8. Alexandria (Va.)—
Economic conditions—18th century. 9. Chesapeake Bay Region (Md. and Va.)—
Economic conditions—18th century. 10. Capitalism—Social aspects—United States—
History—18th century. I. Title.

  F187.C5C83 2008
  975.5'1803—dc22   2008019995

Printed in the United States of America

∞™ The paper used in this publication meets the minimum requirements of American
National Standard for Information Sciences—Permanence of Paper for Printed Library
Materials, ANSI/NISO Z39.48-1992.

Contents

Preface

I am grateful for the opportunities I have been given to work on such interesting archaeological projects. This work owes great intellectual debt to Mark Leone, who facilitated all my work in Annapolis and has been a strong supporter of my ideas. The 99 Main Street property was excavated by Archaeology in Annapolis, the program created and directed by Mark Leone, and the planning, access, and budget were all provided by Leone through the Historic Annapolis Foundation. Several fieldschool students from the University of Maryland extended their summers excavating at the site after the fieldschool was finished, which was quite helpful.

Likewise URS Corporation deserves major acknowledgement. The Jamieson's Bakery was excavated as part of the Lee Street Archaeological Project by URS Corporation in conjunction with Alexandria Archaeology. The final phase of excavations at 99 Main Street was conducted through URS, and the research on Piscataway is based on a series of excavations in the area of Piscataway Village by URS. A handful of students from the University of Maryland went back and forth working both at 99 Main Street and Piscataway. The work at Lee Street was conducted under the direction of Pam Cressey of Alexandria Archaeology, and carried out by a URS field crew directed by Philip Hill, along with many volunteers.

The historical research for these projects was conducted at the Alexandria Library, the Historic Annapolis Foundation, the Maryland State Archives in

Annapolis, the Maryland Historical Trust, the University of Maryland at College Park, and the John D. Rockefeller Jr. Library at Colonial Williamsburg. Many thanks to Rita and the staff at the Alexandria Library Special Collections. Most photographs were taken by myself, and the plan maps showing archaeological features were created using CorelDRAW. Will Mumford was a friendly advisor and graciously allowed me to publish on his work at Cornhill Street, for which I am especially thankful.

This book is expanded from an invited evening lecture presented at the William Paca House in 2005 and sponsored by the Historic Annapolis Foundation. A detailed version of the thesis on economic impacts was presented at the 40th Annual Meeting of the Society for Historical Archaeology in Williamsburg, Virginia, in a session honoring the career of archaeologist Nan Rothschild. You can never fully repay your professors in kind for what they teach you. This book is one token of my appreciation for Nan and the Columbia University anthropology program.

1

Introduction

"It's the economy, stupid!"

James Carville, advisor to President Bill Clinton

This book is an explanation of the social relations of production that accompanied economic growth prior to and after the American Revolution. The focus is the Chesapeake Bay tidewater areas of Virginia and Maryland from about 1720 to 1850. The main data are the history and archaeology of four bakers and their bakeries, with examples from a handful of other archeological sites as well. Baking was one of a number of production industries carried out in Chesapeake urban centers that became increasingly specialized over time as populations and market systems grew. Baking was initially a task carried out by individual artisan craftsmen. Over time, however, the structure of the economy as well as the production processes of baking both changed, reorganized for more intensive and larger scales of operation, and eventually mechanized. The same process can be applied to many industries, and was intrinsic to the growth of urban centers in the Americas.

Communities are often defined and shaped by what they do. Colonial ideology has been a central focus of study in historical archaeology, especially with regard to social elites and how their conceptions of science, philosophy, and culture shaped colonial settlements (e.g., Deetz 1977; Leone 2005). Ideological changes in the eighteenth and early nineteenth centuries were accompanied by corollary developments in the worldwide economy, which are

1

examined here. Among working people, the organization of labor within production and distribution systems shaped their daily lives. Urban archaeology can provide considerable evidence about urban workers and business organization, details that were often not recorded by public history. This research focuses on urban social changes that accompanied American economic growth before and after the Revolutionary War. A central dynamic to this discussion is the role of production, and decisions made by individuals about business and labor practices within a rapidly changing economy.

The process of economic growth and industrialization in America has always been closely linked with class struggle. In the late eighteenth century, as the scale of economic activity in the Chesapeake area grew, the prominent merchants vied with the artisan craftsmen over control of production systems. The result was the development of a managerial or middle class who established new modes of labor and production organization within an expanding economic framework. This study documents the stages of growth for urban production systems. There is a focus on the drive of the production sector of society—the urban "middle class"—and how their organization of labor, advocacy of their trades, and mechanization of activities complemented political and mercantile interests to lay the groundwork for increased capitalist industrialization.

Studies of past economic processes must first address the question of whether the economy is a product of society, or conversely if society is a product of an overarching economy. There can be no consideration of causality without such a discussion, and only limited or one-dimensional understanding of the circumstances. Where does *the economy* start and stop? Is there a beginning and end point? By the twentieth century this question becomes a classic Zen koan, or tautological exercise, that appears to have no end or answer. We are part of the economy and it is part of us. In modern American society it is crass to speak of money, but when pressed to make decisions our actions are strongly influenced by economic parameters. Most of us don't control macroeconomic forces, yet our own individual parts contribute to the whole of the system. Obviously economy is very important to society, and yet we find it hard to say exactly what that role is and how the different variables are related. Terminology such as *the invisible hand* and *voodoo economics* reflect the mysterious and complex nature of capitalism. Issues that are hard to describe in the present are even more difficult when studying them in the past.

Charting the developmental stages of economic systems over time in order to see how and when certain activities developed can help us understand their associations.

The research of social scientists—historians, economists, and anthropologists—looks to the human impacts as a way to characterize individual actions and the development and effects of systemic processes. Economists might ask, "Where is the wealth and money coming from, and where is it going to"; the historians might say, "What records can we find that will begin to build a social context of interpretation"; and the historical anthropologist might ask, "How were people's actions or behavior shaped by opportunity, and how did they develop into patterns and traditions?" These are all primary underlying themes to this work. They are put into action through production, exchange, and consumption, the economic terms for various types of social interaction and activity. In the past, much of that social and economic interaction took place at the level of the community—that is, above the scale of the individual or household but below the scale of the city or state polity. For urban archaeologists, economic models can provide an effective framework of interaction in which to evaluate individuals and their dealings within a community context.

This research investigates the personal reactions of bakers to economic growth by looking at the archaeological correlates left behind in two Chesapeake urban centers, Annapolis, Maryland, and Alexandria, Virginia (figure 1.1). The goal is to highlight the underlying political-economic relationships that enabled, oriented, and constrained the growth of these local towns (Wolf 1982). To do this the book centers on a single industry—baking—as well as a critical time in American history, the early eighteenth to mid-nineteenth centuries. In the center of that period, in 1776, the thirteen American colonies declared independence from Britain. This discussion, then, is set within the global context of expanding world markets, political rivalries, and capitalist developments. In economic terms, this was a time when British colonial controls on American economic activities were replaced with more localized controls. Globally, the market economic system based on agriculture and mercantile trade activity evolved toward capitalism and heavy investments in manufacturing processes.

All of this manifested itself in unique ways in the local production systems of the greater Annapolis and Alexandria region in colonial and early Federal

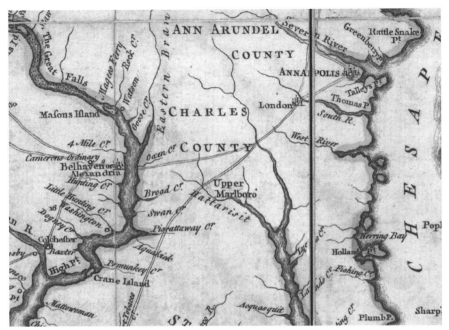

Figure 1.1.
Map of Western Chesapeake Bay and Potomac River Valley showing towns in 1755
(Fry and Jefferson 1755).

periods. The information presented here draws from numerous archaeological excavations in Maryland and Virginia, the area stretching from the tidal Potomac River Valley across to Annapolis and the western shore of the Chesapeake Bay. Urban manufacturing is discussed in relation to two bakeries from Annapolis and two generations of a baking family from Alexandria. Research at these sites provides artifacts and historical details of the scale, organization, and process of urban manufacturing. These are coupled with a discussion of the origins of the American financial system and its Scottish influences. Excavations at two locations, the Chalmers Mint in Annapolis and Piscataway Village just downriver from Alexandria, provide information with which to characterize systemic economic changes.

This book takes a diachronic perspective, looking at transformations over time and highlighting elements of variation in craft production that affected urban populations in the Chesapeake region. It is, by extension, an example of the development of capitalism in the mid-Atlantic United States. Production was closely intertwined with class differentiation, urban social systems, economic developments, and factional struggles. In broad terms, the social changes at this time can be characterized as a period when traditional artisan craftsmen expanded a market economy and competed with the merchant class, who believed they were the ones who should retain control of the economy and assume control over manufacturing. Archaeological research from two pivotal colonial Chesapeake towns reveals the context of people, activities, and settings for urban economic development.

ECONOMIC TRANSFORMATIONS

Baking has been a basic human activity for thousands of years and was arguably a part of every urban development worldwide. The story of the urban baking process in the eighteenth and nineteenth centuries is predictable, and the ending is already known. In the early eighteenth century when the population densities in colonial Chesapeake settlements were low, baking was a household tradecraft that provided subsistence but was difficult to maintain as a viable business outside of large population centers. By the mid-nineteenth century, baking had become a mechanized industry carried out in factories like most large-scale production. The evolution of the process between those two polar examples was a function of social, economic, and political changes that were taking place throughout the trans-Atlantic trading centers.

As colonial ports, Annapolis and Alexandria acted as the interface of global and local processes. Substantive economic changes took place in these towns between the 1760s and 1790s. The American war for independence from Britain began with the Declaration of Independence in 1776 and it was complete by 1782. With that, the residents of Maryland and Virginia went from being a collection of expatriate colonial consumers to a unified nation of producers (Kulikoff 2000). Taking an economic perspective on the process, historians have dubbed the phenomenon a *market revolution* (Breen 2004; Henretta 1998; Peskin 2003; Sellers 1991).

Prior to the American Revolution, England sat as the manufacturing center of its colonial empire. Several acts passed by the British Parliament in the seventeenth and eighteenth centuries, such as the Navigation Act and the Hat Act, were designed to thwart large-scale manufacturing in the American colonies, making it essentially illegal (Coulter 1944; Dawley 1976). The 1660

Navigation Act enumerated a list of commodities that colonists had to send directly to the British Isles. Chief among them were tobacco, sugar, and flour. Legislation like the Navigation Act put England at the center of an extractive colonial economy. Raw materials were sent directly to Britain, and manufactured products made their way back to the colonies for sale (Chayanov 1966; Soltow 1959; Wallerstein 1989). Eighteenth-century England was at the forefront of manufacturing, and the American standard of living was dependent on those manufactured goods. The legal codes ensured Great Britain a central place in this global economy by which they could tax goods and services, monitor mercantile trade, and share in the proceeds of sales. This system was tolerated in the American colonies because there was plenty of money to be made through agricultural pursuits (Bridenbaugh 1950; Kulikoff 2000).

American colonists, however, were merely accommodating those prohibitions. They were consumers of British import goods but their distance from London allowed some leeway for a low level of domestic production. Artisan craftsmen operated on a local and individual basis, maintaining household workshops where they practiced their crafts, relying on small-scale local market systems to obtain raw materials and to distribute their products (Walsh et al. 1997). Day-to-day items of life such as groceries were generally obtained on credit, to be paid off later with tobacco notes or some other item of value paid either directly to the individual, to a community check station or trader, or maybe at some other agreed-upon business (Kulikoff 1993). In localized urban areas, artisan craftsmen were entrepreneurs who could practice their crafts at a small but effective scale to sustain economic viability. They thrived in relation to both the restrictions and temptations of the growing world economy. In the decades before the Revolution, an increasing number of American colonists were producers whose actions seemed restrained by the political parameters.

Under the colonial system, the merchants conducting the trans-Atlantic trading of materials and products often became wealthy. They constituted a social elite class as a result of their wealth, if not for their services. Despite their financial successes, one of the most prominent economic philosophers of the day, the Edinburgh scholar Adam Smith, thought merchants to be among the most loathsome members of society. Merchants didn't actually produce anything, and in Smith's view were not to be trusted (Smith [1776] 2000). In Chesapeake towns the concept of political independence from England presented a challenge to the merchants' position in the economic and social order. Political independence translated into separation from the manufacturing center, as well as angering a trading ally. The loss of imports necessitated a relatively swift progression in Chesapeake towns in the third quarter of the eighteenth century from traditional *household* production to larger *workshop* factories that could accommodate a regional consumer base.

By the 1760s, nonimportation petitions were being circulated in most colonial cities in America, including Annapolis and Alexandria. As dissatisfaction with British rule increased, many craftsmen flaunted the rules and expanded their manufacturing. These renegade craftsmen tended to be located in urban settings, which had the necessary elements to carry out manufacturing. The colonial towns had active distribution networks that could supply raw materials, and the towns had adequate opportunity for sales. The previous system of merchant import/export business dwindled as overseas trade was frowned upon. Sentiments against merchant tyranny and royal taxes grew steadily into the 1770s. Much of that sentiment was a dislike of British taxes on manufactured goods and imports, but some was directed at the merchants themselves. The following antimerchant passage ran in the *Virginia Gazette* in 1771:

> In these times of liberty and patriotism I have expected to see the tyranny of merchants opposed. . . . We all know that we are slaves to the power of the merchants: For who can truly say he is free, when there is a fixed price set upon his tobacco, and the goods he purchases, at rates he does not like? Long custom makes that seem tolerable, which in reality is a great imposition; . . . What a blind infatuated multitude we must be to suffer those, who ought to be dependent on us, to become our masters?
> *Virginia Gazette*, October 31, 1771 (cited in Soltow 1959)

With American independence, the system was different. After the Revolutionary War, the lower- and middle-class artisan craftsmen were at the center of a new economy that was reinventing itself. That shift had started in the production sector. Artisan craftsmen were the ones who challenged the administrative directives of London and expanded their businesses prior to the war. Wartime production was a lucrative process that benefitted many craftsmen and facilitated the war effort. With a reduction in imported goods, the urban artisan craftsmen who had operated essentially outside the international trade system had to *grow* their production. Many made nice profits during the war.

Increasingly freed from British restrictions, artisan craftsmen of the tidewater Chesapeake area increased production and expanded the scale of their operations by taking on apprentices and enlarging their workshops. Growth in local production also included the expansion of urban labor markets and the strengthening of organized trade groups among the artisan craftsmen. It was termed a *market revolution* as it was predicated on the rise of local market production forces to accommodate political independence (Breen 2004; Peskin 2003; Sellers 1994; Wilentz 1984).

The unrestrained growth of urban craft businesses did not continue for long. The prevailing economic theories of Adam Smith espousing free trade were replaced in the 1780s and 1790s with those of the American statesman Alexander Hamilton. This was as much a function of global economics as it was a local business decision. Hamilton strongly believed that the nascent United States needed a strong manufacturing base, but he believed that as a new country trying to compete with established European powers, the only way to accomplish this was through heavy federal government involvement. The new U.S. government established a system designed to help critical industries grow quickly, and set up tariffs to "protect" American producers from overseas competition. The process is often called *neomercantilism*, a term describing political policies that favor controls over trade, markets, and capital to encourage exportation. Within a few years of the conclusion of the Revolution, artisan craftsmen found their trades taxed by the new U.S. government who wanted to promote industry but needed the income that regulation of these trades would bring. The biggest predicament for the artisan craftsmen, however, was general resentment among the once powerful merchant/traders (Braudel 1979; Dawley 1976).

The position of this book is that emerging urban economies were being driven by producers under colonial rule and for a short while after independence. Artisan craftsmen expanded their businesses on principles of enlightened self-interest. There was opportunity for additional income through growth and they acted on it. That self-initiative represents an agency-oriented growth of economic production processes. American independence from Britain was facilitated by these urban producers who took it upon themselves to increase production and distribution of their crafts. However, the success of the craftsmen was ultimately co-opted by more wealthy and politically powerful class factions who wanted to regain control of the economy after the

Revolution. This was a class struggle, based largely on economic primacy, and the catch was that the structure of both the economy and society were changing in response.

This study strives for a multidisciplinary perspective on the issue of manufacturing and urban change. Archaeological studies related to economic behaviors generally focus on consumerism as a means of evaluating class and status differences within a population (Gibb 1996; Spencer-Wood 1987). Consumer decisions highlight personal purchasing choices, but tend to do so from within a given structural perspective. It is true that consumer decisions fed back into production, but overall the American economy itself was evolving and growing, and in urban areas this was largely based on production-based decisions like labor availability, distribution networks, and political regulations. Studies of colonial era production have generally focused on the organization of agriculture, which was the primary mode of production across the American colonies. The tobacco trade and the practice of slavery fostered a dichotomous social context of wealthy planters and poor landless laborers throughout much of the countryside. The power relationships in those settings, especially of slaves and their owners, placed immense limitations on the creative and entrepreneurial activities of the powerless (Orser 1988; Singleton 1985; Vlach 1993; Wilkie 2000). In contrast, artisan craftsmen of late eighteenth and early nineteenth century Chesapeake towns were relatively free actors. Their motivations and opportunities progressed and expanded over time as they redefined themselves and their businesses in relation to changing economic forces of a world market and its localized impacts. Issues of slave and indentured labor remained central to urban production, and many urban tradecrafts used enslaved and indentured labor, but in their own unique ways. Likewise the process of expanding production contained elements of power struggle, coercion, and bias. Those struggles, however, were between the socioeconomic status of the merchant classes, who had gained considerable wealth from overseas trade, and the working artisan craftsmen who saw the potential to gain a majority of that market.

PRODUCTION ORGANIZATION FROM COLONY TO NATION

This is a work of historical archaeology, and the premise of the discipline is commonly acknowledged as the archaeology of capitalism (Leone 1984; Johnson 1996; Paynter 1988). The terms *capitalism*, as well as *Industrial Revolution*, have accrued complex meanings within our modern terminology that can be misleading. The concept of an industrial revolution in America has come to describe the emergence of industrialized manufacturing as an economic mode of production after the Revolutionary War. Capitalism has come to be seen as the economy of an industrialized society. A central goal of studying the past is to "unpack" the individual processes and events that comprise sweeping historical movements in order to explore in more depth the relationships of the variables and their effects on developments. Central elements of both industrialization and capitalism were in place before the Revolution, and provided a foundation for further changes afterward.

Both capitalism and the industrial revolution are broadly defined phenomena. There is analytical value in studying them as objectified eras in history, but it must be recognized that there was a time before these systemic categories had come into existence. The term *capitalism* is simply the ex post facto name given to an economic system based on reinvestment of capital resources in the production process. The term *industrial revolution* has long been a catch-all phrase to describe large-scale mechanization of production processes in the mid-nineteenth century. Many of the underlying social and economic changes that reshaped the American economic system and enabled labor reorganization and mechanization originated in the eighteenth century as struggles between political and class factions. That process involved the people and institutions that would become the foundations of industrialism—the owners, managers, and laborers. It was also the foundation of capitalism as an economic process. There was accumulation and polarization of wealth across classes, and an alignment of factors that would facilitate reinvestment into manufacturing.

In urban settings, economic transactions were paramount and the politics associated with them complex (Matthews 2001; Rothschild 1990; Wilkie 2004). Cultural traditions were more diverse and influential in American urban settings than in rural ones. As the center of merchant trading activities, it was the urbanized towns and cities where financial institutions grew and where creative financial instruments were tested. Likewise, the East Coast urban ports, initially transshipment points for bulk raw materials, became centers of production and nodes of exchange. Capital investments in production began with urban trades, and that is where concepts for reorganizing administration and labor within production and distribution processes were generated. In the Chesapeake tidewater setting, that growth reflects the dialectic relationships between individual agency and global economy (Roseberry 1988; Wilkie and Bartoy 2000).

In the mid-eighteenth century, the total populations of Annapolis and Alexandria weren't more than a couple thousand people each (e.g., Leone 2005). It is clear that the actions of individual craftsmen were significant to the social dynamics of these towns. It is also clear that those artisan craftsmen responded to systemic structures like commodity values and global markets. Choices were made by individual craft producers who continuously positioned themselves and their social roles with respect to economic opportunities, first within the British colonial system and later within the new American system (Polanyi 1944; Spencer-Wood 1987).

Baking was a typical urban trade activity carried out in most towns. In Annapolis, the 99 Main Street bakeries—actually two different bakeries built in the same location—were utilized by several different individuals throughout the eighteenth century. The first bakery produced ship's bread, making a business supporting the extensive activities of the port of Annapolis. That bakery burned in 1790, and an upgraded version was built overtop the ruins to resume its business. In Alexandria, the Jamiesons were a baking family who operated numerous bakery businesses over two generations. From the 1780s to the 1850s the Jamiesons expanded their baking enterprises from a domestic industry into a large mechanized business that shipped crackers to overseas markets. Bakers comprised a distinctive group of people, and bakeries required some unique business characteristics. Some studies consider baking to be part of the service economy (e.g., Papenfuse 1975), but baking was a production task that required a certain amount of skilled knowledge on the part of the individual as well as specialized facilities and tools. It is discussed here as a craft, and the bakeries treated as craft workshops. The combination of examples from Annapolis and Alexandria follow each other sequentially in time and provide an illustration of incremental growth within an industry. Increasing economic specialization in the eighteenth century led ultimately to substantive economic changes in the 1790s and an era of industrial production by the mid-nineteenth century.

Urban economics from the eighteenth and nineteenth centuries can be difficult to study because the details of urban settlements were volatile. Economic factors changed precipitously between different times and places, as did intellectual philosophies and urban social movements. Accompanying the growth in production, the Chesapeake tidewater area saw the development of new modes of finance and evolving systems of payment for goods and services. A challenge to understanding these historical events is to adequately contextualize the actual transaction methods in use, which were not always clear and which leave room for interpretation. Monetary purchases with currency, which is the prevailing custom today, was the least common form of transaction. Spanish coins were the most common hard currency in the Chesapeake region in colonial times, but even they were rare. Elaborate credit systems allowed business to take place with very little cash in circulation. What I call credit was actually a barter system in which consumers had running tabs at stores, and fulfilled payments with other goods at certain times of the year. The credit system prior to the Revolution facilitated commodity exchanges, but relied heavily on trust that an eventual payment would be forthcoming. The towns provided an effective sized social unit within which these "trust economies" of credit could operate.

By the time independence was declared in 1776, this exchange and barter system was complex. In the Chesapeake tidewater area much of it was being managed by a distinct group of professionals. Scottish merchant firms had established general stores that functioned like community banks. These firms, who traded commodities between continents before the Revolution, transformed themselves into financial managers afterwards. The British pound and Spanish milled dollar, the currencies of choice before the Revolution, were replaced with U.S. dollars as well as new American banking and tax systems. In Annapolis, a local goldsmith started minting his own coins in 1783. At the same time, the Scottish trading firm of John Glassford & Company, with branch stores along the Potomac and other Chesapeake tributaries, offered quasi-banking services like depository notes and lines of credit that enabled the growth of urban production and changed the nature of the region's economy.

MARKETS AND CAPITALISM

Economic development of tidewater Chesapeake has been a popular theme of study for many disciplines interested in the American past. This book draws from anthropology and history, with an element of economics. Economic themes are generally viewed by social scientists as primary causal mechanisms

affecting other institutions (Leone 1995, Wallerstein 1989). New cultural practices evolved rapidly in the colonial period in concert with economic opportunities and emerging industry (Kulikoff 1979, 1986). There is considerable
historical evidence with which to understand macroeconomic processes, and
historians have pieced together many aspects of economic development in
Annapolis and Alexandria (Duffy 1965; Hardy 1999; Hurst 1991; Papenfuse
1975; Sharrer 1977; Shephard 1985). Colonial merchants who conducted international business left ledger books, receipts, and correspondence that offer
historic documentation of the growth of international banking and trade industries. Archaeology is crucial to understanding smaller scale and local economic processes that were more ad hoc and fluid.

In his seminal article "A Historical Archaeology of Capitalism," Leone
(1995) effectively outlines how class and power differences were causal in the
historical development of the Chesapeake. The present discussion adds to that
work by examining details of the socioeconomic growth that constrained
working people and, by extension, enhanced social and status inequalities in
the transition between market and capitalist economic systems. Many aspects
of daily social life were orchestrated to accommodate these economic systems.

In the 1600s and early 1700s colonial America lived predominantly under
an extractive colonialist economy that dovetailed with an international market system of trade (Gibb 1996; Henretta 1998; Wallerstein 1974, 1976; Wolf
1982). The earliest European settlements in the Chesapeake region were
founded as business ventures, and I consider most of that period a time of *extractive colonial* economy (table 1.1). Early colonists who were socially connected received land grants, while individual settlers, who were sometimes
indentured and often of limited means, were concerned with frontier subsistence and living off the land. The goal was to make a quick profit from tobacco
(Kulikoff 1986; Walsh 1977).

**Table 1.1. Successive stages of economic development for the
Chesapeake economy. Based on Henretta (1998) and personal opinion.**

Economic system	Dates
Extractive colonial	1607–1720
Subsistence-plus	1720–1760
Market (mercantile)	1760–1783
Proto-capitalism (neomercantilism)	1784–~1830
Capitalism (with cash economy but no gold standard)	1830–1875

The time period from 1720 to 1850 saw the American economic system transform, and it can be classified into several different stages. By the 1720s many Chesapeake settlements were well established, and with the growth of global commodity markets, even the small individual planters became focused primarily on production for the market (Price 1995). These planters maintained an agrarian mode of production and sold parts of their yield to nearby warehouses that shipped them to Europe. Those transshipment points often developed into towns, although not all and not very quickly. I have called this the *subsistence-plus* economy, after Henretta (1998), in that it involved subsistence agriculture plus a little extra. This is not a neat category, but for lack of a better term, subsistence-plus describes the general economic strategy of the time, in which most individuals made a living plus a little more.

For about two decades prior to the Revolution, the Chesapeake region was heavily involved in a *market* economy. Sometimes called the mercantile economy, the market economy was a precapitalist economy driven largely by the activities of merchant traders who shipped agricultural products like tobacco and wheat flour from eastern American ports to European markets. In return they got refined products like dishware for table settings, liquors, and textiles. London trading houses would sometimes buy crops on consignment and have them shipped. In other cases the shippers would front the cost of buying the crops and transporting them, assessing a "middle man" fee. The London merchants found easy sales in the American colonies. There was little risk in sending a collection of finished products to American retailers, and the tobacco they received in return they could sell to France (Price 1987). This market system was the precursor to a *capitalist* system.

The trans-Atlantic market system had interesting implications for local economic activities in the colonies. In the Chesapeake region most transactions were barter, or calculated exchanges. Hard currency was in short supply in the American colonies, and systems of exchange and credit, nested within localized systems of production and distribution, formed the structure of economic interactions, especially in urban settings. Day-to-day sales in Annapolis and Alexandria were carried out with consideration of, but separate from, a monetary system (Gibb 1996; Prattis 1987; Spencer-Wood 1987). The Spanish milled dollar and British pound provided overarching benchmarks by which values were assigned to products, but there was rarely any use of the currencies themselves. For the planters and craftsmen a surplus value was gained through exchange, which at the large scale meant the transportation of their products to locations of high demand. On the local scale the process of adding value meant products created by highly skilled and specialized craftsmen. Social conceptions of wealth, property, land, and labor were somewhat more organic and direct under the market economy than they would become under capitalism (e.g., Gibb 1996; Wallerstein 1974).

COLONIAL SOCIOECONOMICS

It is clear from history that there were transformations in the Chesapeake economy, but why and how those changes took place is debatable. In terms of disciplinary perspectives, economists apply different theoretical models to people than do anthropologists. From an anthropological perspective, people and their cultural patterns are the focus. Underlying connections between people and culture reveal insights into personal choice, or individual agency. The economist's term for agency is *rational choice*. Microeconomic theory of rational choice by consumers explains small-scale and short-term decisions. Microeconomics attempts, from the market perspective, to explain why particular economic decisions are reached in conjunction with existing social organization and cultural values (Wilk 1996). The concepts are similar, but not the same. Anthropologists put the emphasis on the cultural elements, trying to understand the values of rational choice by looking at personal needs and desires and the sociocultural elements available for satisfying those needs. Both are looking at the dynamics of how individuals negotiate between self and system with regard to cultural practices and economic activities.

The intersection of cultural and economic issues is often referred to as the *political economy*. In 1749 Adam Smith first offered classes of instruction in political economy in Edinburg (Hollander 1927). It was a concept he built on throughout his academic career, and with his book *The Wealth of Nations*, Smith ([1776] 2000) essentially established economics as a new social science (Hollander 1927; Rothschild 1992). At that time Smith meant political economy as the politics of commercial and economic life, and did so from the perspective of how best to administer the resources of a nation. Politics in those days was synonymous with economics. The intellectual ideas of political freedom were somewhat new, and the concept that there could be economic freedoms separate from political freedom had not yet emerged in Smith's time (Rothschild 1992). Writing a century later, Karl Marx's ([1867] 1990) tome

Capital extended the effects of political economy to nearly all social relations of life. The Marxian concept for political economy analyzed modes of production set within the social context of political and economic growth. At the time Marx was writing, capitalism was fully developed, if still new in some places, and he had observed how economic decisions could affect even the most basic functions of life for wage earners. Anthropologists have since come to view the social perspective on that process as the political economy, highlighting the interrelationships of class, status, and political power with larger economic forces (Matthews 2001; Roseberry 1988).

This is a study of urban production, which over time became the focus of more and more political decisions and power struggles. The capitalist economy is when wealth can be reinvested in controlling the means of production (Marx [1867] 1990; Wilk 1996). In other words, capitalism is achieved only when money is returned into enhancing production—or, when the money is capitalized through investment. The American market economy of the eighteenth century had a monetary backing in the British pound, but maintained many informal elements of earlier economic systems. The day-to-day operations of urban society were carried out largely as processes of reciprocity and exchange (e.g., Sahlins 1972). This was a precapitalist economy linked to international trade, not investments in production margins. The price of traded commodities was used to assign values to goods and services at the local scale, even though little money exchanged hands (Braudel 1979). There was precious little production, and it was simplistic. The structure was not in place for investment and there was little need for any as long as European traders continued to operate. The onset of capitalism was facilitated by a rise in domestic production and the ability to purchase specialized machines and facilities to enhance production. The threshold event for having capitalism, however, is generally seen as the ability to purchase labor power with money so as to intensify production activities (Marx [1867] 1990; Wolf 1982).

The research presented here draws from Marx ([1867] 1990), Polanyi (1944), and others who have examined the ownership and organization of production in the nineteenth century. Capitalism brought about such drastic changes to society that Polanyi (1944) labeled it "the great transformation." The transition from an agricultural economy to a manufacturing economy varied in each place it occurred, but most historians reiterate that it was in fact a great transformation (Wilentz 1984). Polanyi's study examined capitalism in Britain, mostly the textile industry, and discussed the development of manufacturing in relation to the origins of what he called the three false commodities: land, labor, and money. None of these three things need to be produced, as in a factory. However, only when society allowed them to be bought and sold could capitalism succeed. The enclosure and privatization of land began in Britain in the late Middle Ages, and the monetary system based on the British pound has an equally extensive history. The last false commodity to fall into place in Britain was the free labor market, in which an individual's labor could be purchased with wages but those individuals were free to choose where and at what value they would work.

From the founding of the American colonies, private land tenure was always the practice. Land was granted by royals to colonial proprietors and settlers, who subsequently bought and sold parcels among themselves regularly. American colonists were likewise versed in European monetary systems, using numerous currencies and tolerating their shifting utility and value. Because of the lack of hard currency in colonial America, most urban areas that appeared to use the British monetary system developed secondary economic systems that focused on credit and exchange. Nevertheless, they were seen to be a monetary society with the pound as their standard. As was the case in Britain, the commodification of labor and the development of a free labor market were the last of the variables of a capitalist economy, the false commodities so to speak, to develop in America.

Eric Wolf (1982) has made a significant contribution to anthropological study of labor organization by emphasizing the contrast between *work* and *labor* within a growing economic dynamic. In general, within precapitalist market economies a skilled craftsman worked toward creating products that had social value. The value was based on the skill and workmanship that went into the products, and those products were used to remunerate other costs that the worker incurred within the society (Wallerstein 1976; Wilk 1996). In that system the worker made their own decisions, and their actions were qualitatively related to their products and to production in general. I refer to those people as *artisan craftsmen* because of the inherent skills they applied to their products. In contrast, within capitalist economies labor is separated out as an interchangeable commodity unto itself. Instead of applying skills to a product, a person's time is purchased and deployed strategically toward specific production tasks. This was "socially deployed" labor, in the sense that it was bought with money and directed toward some goal that the buyer decided. Capital investments in production found it useful to itemize and standardize manufacturing processes so that specialized skills were less and less necessary. With that, manufacturers could utilize the widest pool of labor available, and production was not limited by the availability of special skills. Ownership of land, equipment, and labor took on new social meanings when they could be controlled or deployed by someone else, and became more related to the process of production instead of to the products themselves (Polanyi 1944, 1957). The ability to purchase labor time using money, which effectively reduced skilled *work* into commoditized *labor*, marks an evolutionary milestone in production organization and consequently within the social structure of less affluent classes who would come to be known as the working class.

A key element of labor studies in America in the eighteenth and nineteenth centuries is the existence of slavery. The tobacco trade in Virginia and Maryland was a leading contributor in the rise of enslaved labor in the Chesapeake region. Plantations of the eighteenth century required large amounts of human labor to be cost effective. Periodic declines in prices on the world markets meant that crops such as tobacco could only stay profitable if their production was carried out with enslaved labor (Kulikoff 1986), resulting in a dependency of the agrarian system on slavery. Slavery is often classified as the southern labor system of the United States centered on plantation agriculture, whereas the development of urban factories is often generalized as the northern system. The mid-Atlantic area of Annapolis and Alexandria was the literal boundary of north and south, and this study examines how these two contrasted modes of production, enslaved labor and urban production, became blended. The employment of enslaved individuals in nonagricultural labor and manufacturing processes resulted from the growth of industry as well as a diversification of farming practices (Jernegan 1978; Newton and Lewis 1978). The cities had a very different history than the plantations. The urban settings of Annapolis and Alexandria actually encouraged freedom (Leone 2005). This book explores, in part, how nonagrarian labor processes developed in urban settings and ultimately contributed to changing intellectual views on slavery, the organization of labor, and the benefits of a free labor market nationwide.

THE 1790 CHANGE

A significant threshold of change was crossed in approximately 1790, when the first traces of an independent American economy began to take hold. It was in that year that the Scottish economist and reigning proponent of un-regulated mercantile trade, Adam Smith, died. With him went his philosophy of economic liberalism, the laissez faire economics based on free trade (Roth-schild 1992). A new era of nationalism in economics was emerging. In the United States, Alexander Hamilton was the treasury secretary, and he is asso-ciated with the general shift toward government interventions on industry and trade. Hamilton wanted to establish a national bank with the goal of transforming America's barter economy and bolstering industry. He was com-missioned by the U.S. House of Representatives in January 1790 to prepare a report on the state of American manufacturing.

Hamilton believed that American technological backwardness stood in the way of industrialization. He identified national power with development of manufacturing. Free trade was a good thing in principle, but just not possible for the politically weak United States (Harlen 1999). Trade monopolies and high shipping tariffs could level the playing field. Hamilton urged Congress to launch an aggressive campaign to acquire Britain's technology (Ben-Atar 1995). Congress refused the plan, opting to make no industrial policy, but did pass the U.S. patent law. In December 1790, Hamilton issued his report on a national bank. His final *Report on Manufacturers* would not emerge until De-cember 1791. As both political and economic policy, the effects of these two reports on burgeoning U.S. business would be profound. In short order, po-litical interests, investments, and power became entangled locally within a na-tional political economy.

The bakeries described in this book reflect the effects of American political economy within towns. The American Revolution had disrupted trade for merchants, and that was compounded by the European wars of the 1790s, which disrupted continental markets for all but the best Chesapeake tobacco (Papenfuse 1975). This was another blow to the merchants of the Chesapeake region, and most were restless, watching the economic changes and searching out new opportunities. John Davidson was a merchant businessman in An-napolis who had been appointed custom's officer in 1767. He stepped down in 1790 because there was so little trade there, and there was no point in carry-ing on (Cuddy and Leone 2008). Economically speaking, in 1790, and a little before and after, the American economy was on hold (McCusker and Menard 1985). Coincidentally, there were two bakery fires, one in Annapolis in 1790 and one in Alexandria in 1795. I suggest here that fires in bakeries and other workshops in the 1790s were not all accidental. Instead, I am suggesting here that fire was being used criminally and tactically in cities up and down the East Coast as a first step toward shifting control of economic processes away from traditional artisan craftsmen and back to merchants. Economic and political policies were being formulated in the 1790s but implementation was slow, times were difficult, and it wasn't at all clear how it would work out.

ARCHAEOLOGICAL EVIDENCE

The locations discussed in this book have been intensely researched, both historically and archaeologically. Most people are familiar with history, but not as much with how archaeological evidence complements it. Some elements of the past were documented historically, but not all and not evenly. There is a record of industrialism in America, but this book attempts to understand the events that preceded industrialism, some of which were subtle local occurrences. Archaeological materials provide another method for understanding people, places, and events of the past, sometimes where historical documentation is lacking and sometimes in conjunction with documentary evidence. Colonial record-keeping in Maryland and Virginia included such important data as births and deaths, population censuses, and tax assessments. The context of an archaeological site and its artifacts comprise remnants of past activities and processes.

On historical sites, archaeological materials—the artifacts and features—represent both consumption and production activities, and in this case urban growth in general. Artifacts described in this book have been classified as closely as possible into the categories established by South (1977), which are a combination of the functional use of objects and their material type. This book is largely urban archaeology, and in general architectural materials are the most common class of artifact recovered in cities. Household and kitchen items make up the next largest class, and then hardware and miscellaneous items. Ceramics are the favorite of the archaeologist, since the dates of their production and trade are well known. Many ceramics were used in the baking business, but most were functional vessels with few distinguishing characteristics. Personal items were also found at all the sites. Items such as buttons and the broken stems and bowls from tobacco pipes were ubiquitous. Most pipes were the British-made ball clay type, but with some locally made exceptions.

The artifacts and features of an archaeological site rarely have individual value. Instead they provide indications of patterns that reflect broad uses of materials and of repeated activities. The archaeological data described here was used in several ways for analysis. Excavated architectural remains, including foundation walls, wells, and ovens, provide insight into the structure and layout of the various baking facilities. Overall, they provide indications of scale and complexity of the bakery business. Some of what was excavated is indicative of events or processes, like the mortar pit for construction of the 99 Main Street building, or the sooty black stains from fires. The artifacts that weren't architectural were mostly pottery but also other small objects of daily life. Those objects reflect generally on the activities that were conducted in those areas, and to some extent provide indications of the socioeconomic status of the people and businesses.

Archaeological evidence is most valuable in its ability to establish contexts of setting, time, and place. A considerable amount of historical research is presented here, both from primary and secondary documentary sources. The different forms of archaeological data discussed, in conjunction with the historical information, allow for an interpolation of the context of the sites and the broad social patterns and trends that they represent. Brief discussions of ceramics are presented in the chapters, since ceramics were instrumental in regard to the dating of sites, and because those data are meaningful for other archaeologists doing similar work. In general, this work presents the archaeological data in an interpreted format as part of the overall discussion.

URBAN GEOGRAPHY OF TIDEWATER CHESAPEAKE

The Chesapeake Bay tidewater area is a distinctive environmental phenomenon and its physical characteristics contributed greatly to its cultural development. The Chesapeake Bay is the largest estuary in the United States. The bay and its tributaries cover more than 4,500 square miles, or 41 million acres, and drain a 64,000 square mile watershed stretching from New York to North Carolina. It is supplied by approximately 150 rivers, streams, and creeks that flow into it, which contain approximately 11,700 miles of shoreline (Ernst 2003). Much of the area's waters fluctuate with the ocean's tides, producing wide navigable rivers, coves, and inlets, and giving the area the *tidewater* name. The bay and its tributaries were the central focus of early colonial settlement. Captain

John Smith and the first European settlers were impressed with the bay's abundant marine resources. Smith and the other seventeenth-century colonists survived by learning the region's secrets from the Native Americans, and a syncretic culture developed blending European, African, and Native American traditions.

As neighboring colonies, Maryland and Virginia shared a regional cultural development that centered on the tobacco trade, the ecology of the Chesapeake, and a largely Scottish heritage of their founding European populations (Kulikoff 1986; Middleton 1984; Papenfuse 1975). The many waterways of the bay's tributaries were the roads and highways of the seventeenth and eighteenth centuries. Colonists traveled by boat and migration and trade followed these routes. Annapolis is situated on the open bay, at the mouth of the Severn River and Spa Creek. In 1670, Thomas Todd laid out 120 acres north of Spa Creek (Luckenbach 1995; Moss 1976; Ware 1990). He set up a boatyard near Acton's Cove and the site came to be known as *Todd's Landing* or *Todd's Harbor* (Ware 1990:68). Robert Proctor also patented land at the mouth of Spa Creek (Moss 1976), and "the Towne land at Proctors" gradually became known as "Anne Arundel Towne" (Ware 1990:68). The town became an official port of entry for the tobacco trade in 1683, and was renamed Arundelton. During that same year, the town's commissioners were authorized to purchase one hundred acres from current landowners. Richard Beard surveyed the city and staked it into one hundred lots, each one acre, with streets, alleys, and open spaces for a church, chapel, market, and other public buildings (Baker 1986; Riley 1901). The development of the town gained momentum when the new royal governor, Sir Francis Nicholson, oversaw the relocation of the colony's capital from St. Mary's City to Arundelton in 1694. Nicholson redesigned the city plan, imposing Baroque design conventions popular in European cities onto Beard's haphazard grid and renaming the city Annapolis (Baker 1986; Leone et al. 1998; Reps 1972; Yentsch 1994).

The location of Alexandria was originally part of a seven hundred acre patent along the Potomac River, due west of Annapolis. The patent was issued to Margaret Brent (1601–1671) of Maryland on September 6, 1654, by Virginia Royal Governor Richard Bennett (Miller 1995). Brent had been promised land in Maryland by Cecil Calvert, the Lord Baltimore, but she ultimately moved fifty miles upriver from St. Mary's City, and to the other side of the river, to the home constructed by her brother Giles near Aquia, Virginia. She repatented her seven hundred acres "in the Freshes of Potomac River beginning at the Mouth of Hunting Creek" in 1662, but Governor Berkeley had also issued an overlapping patent of six thousand acres to Robert Howson, a Welsh sea captain in October 1669 (Miller 1995). Howson quickly resold his real estate to John Alexander on November 13, 1669, for six thousand pounds of crop tobacco. Alexander did not realize that Brent's seven hundred acres were encompassed in his grant, and had to pay for the parcel twice. Upon John Alexander's death, his holdings were devised to his two sons, Robert and Philip, hence the name Alexandria. The Virginia Legislature passed a tobacco inspection act in 1730 that called for the construction of tobacco warehouses along the major tributaries in order that it could be inspected, packed, and shipped to Great Britain. The region near the foot of Oronoco Street became known as Hugh West's Hunting Creek Warehouse and by the early 1740s other English and Scottish merchants including John Pagan, John Carlyle, and William Ramsay had settled there. Since the warehouse site was "the last and best Virginia anchorage for ocean vessels before the Potomac Falls," Lawrence Washington and Lord Thomas Fairfax joined in the ranks of the early traders and petitioned the Virginia General Assembly for the right to establish a town. The Virginia House of Burgesses passed the petition in 1749. Officially called Alexandria, the early hamlet was also known as Belhaven in honor of John Hamilton (1654–1708), the second Lord Belhaven, who had been a patriotic figure in Scotland (Miller 1998).

Annapolis and Alexandria are similar in many ways, including their histories as Chesapeake tobacco ports and their strong Scottish heritage. Both were important colonial Chesapeake towns, and many parallel events took place in both cities. Annapolis was focused toward the open bay and Alexandria on the Potomac River Valley, but the distance between them was only forty miles (64.4 km), a nice day's ride. Business was done in both locations by tradesmen, planters, and merchants, and the newspapers in the two towns often ran the same advertisements, obituaries, and other public notices.

This account starts in Annapolis, which was an eighteenth century economic and political center, and shifts its focus to Alexandria and the Potomac River Valley by the nineteenth century. Far from isolated, the two cities were the larger nodes of activity in a web of plantations and towns that followed the Chesapeake tributaries. They functioned as central places within the cultural, political, and economic development of the region. Other locations are referenced in the chapters, such as the Potomac River towns of Piscataway and Georgetown. These were equally important to the region's growth, but those towns were absorbed by subsequent development; Georgetown was engulfed into the urban sprawl of Washington D.C., while Piscataway, like the towns of Colchester and Dumfries, disappeared, becoming America's lost towns (e.g., Luckenbach 1995; Sprouse 1975; Troupe 1980). By the nineteenth century both Annapolis and Alexandria were referred to as "the ancient city," a common term then for towns that had survived "the great transformation" from an agrarian to an industrial economy (*Philadelphia Inquirer*, August 8, 1863; Riley 1887).

This book is interested in the details of economic change, and how people both caused it and adapted to it. The central interpretive theme elaborated here is the history and archaeology of bakeries as one type of productive industry. Economic change is examined among individual bakers and bakeries in the developing urban settings, giving as much emphasis to the historical research as to the archaeological field data. The archaeology includes various research projects and numerous people and places in Annapolis and Alexandria. The position of artisan craftsmen in the economic context of the eighteenth century was noticeably transformed by 1790 from what it had been prior, and became quite different again in the nineteenth century. This work is divided around that transformation geographically too, beginning with a discussion of Annapolis prior to 1790 and shifting to Alexandria afterwards. The Chalmers Bakery developed in the subsistence economy of eighteenth-century Annapolis. The demise of the Chalmers Bakery and the rise of the Grammar and Jamieson bakeries highlight the upheavals of post-Revolutionary economic and political reorganization at the end of the eighteenth century. The mechanized bakery opened in the nineteenth century by Robert Jamieson signaled the emergence of new capitalists in Alexandria. Looking at these bakeries over time, critical changes are seen in the organization of production systems including labor organization, managerial administration, technological applications, and the financing of various manufacturing businesses. Intertwined in the baking discussion is the role of an emerging and expanding U.S. economy. The Scottish merchants in the Chesapeake, especially John Glassford and Company, played a central role in the development of the region's financial system. A look at the operation of Glassford's stores along the Potomac and the Chalmers Mint site in Annapolis provide the necessary backdrop to understanding economic developments of the Chesapeake culture area.

2

Annapolis and 99 Main Street

Archaeological excavations at 99 Main Street in Annapolis found the artifacts, features, and architectural remains of an early eighteenth-century bakery from the time when Annapolis was an emerging town. Oven-baked goods are a staple food product and they were instrumental in the colonization of the New World. Hard-baked ship's biscuits had a long shelf life that could sustain trans-Atlantic voyages without spoiling. The location of the bakery site in Annapolis is now in the heart of the city's Historic District, a charming collection of buildings that are still laid out according to the original 1695 town plan. Many of the buildings date from the eighteenth century, but few are from the early parts of the century (figure 2.1).

In the early 1700s, Annapolis was a growing port town. Around the waterfront was a collection of "impermanent" post-in-ground wood structures clad in rough wood siding (Carson et al. 1981; Moser et al. 2003). Settlement focused on the waterfront where ships arrived from Jamaica and Barbados, or sometimes directly from Europe. Most early Annapolis residents were somehow involved in the shipping industry, supplying or outfitting the ships themselves, or preparing and processing the goods that would be transported by them. In terms of overall economic activity, the system has been described as subsistence-plus (Henretta 1998), in which people made enough to live from plus a little extra. The bakery at 99 Main Street was probably established, at least initially, to support the shipping trade. Archaeological evidence suggests

FIGURE 2.1.
Picture of the structure at 99 Main Street in Annapolis, built in 1791, with 196 Green
Street protruding off to the right. (Photograph by the author.)

it was constructed in the 1720s. The archaeology presents an example of a typical early eighteenth-century domestic compound with mixed residential and
working areas. However, the shift to more permanent structures and enduring
business was under way.

BEFORE THE UPRISING

In 1683 Annapolis was surveyed and officially made a town. Much of the waterfront land was owned at that time by Robert Proctor (Lindauer 1997).

Proctor died in 1695 and his widow sold the land that would become 99 Main Street to John Wood, whose son, John Wood Jr., sold it to Amos Garrett in 1712.[1] Amos Garrett had been born in England in 1671 and immigrated to Maryland as a free adult by 1701. He served as agent for Sir Thomas Lawrence, one of the richest men in Maryland, and became a merchant planter. Garret also held a number of political offices. He was the first mayor of Annapolis, from 1708 to 1720, was a member of Maryland's Lower House of representatives for many years (1712–1714, 1715, and 1720–1721), and was an Annapolis alderman (c. 1720–1726, Maryland State Archives, n.d.). Garrett never married and had no known progeny. At the time of his death in 1727 he was the richest man in Maryland, with an estate valued at £24,450, which included over eight thousand acres of land, sixty-eight slaves, and ten servants (Papenfuse et al. 1979).

It was during Garrett's ownership of the 99 Main Street property that James Stoddert made his famous 1718 survey of the city. Garrett owned at least nine of the lots on Stoddert's map, and the 99 Main Street lot was labeled as Lot 28 (although it now encompasses part of Lot 32 as well; figures 2.2 and 2.3). Archaeological evidence indicates the earliest constructions on the lot originate from Garrett's time. Lot 28 became the location of the Chalmers Bakery by approximately 1720. At that time Main Street was called Church Street.

FIGURE 2.2.
Stoddart (1718) map of Annapolis.

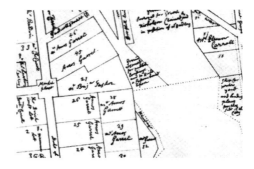

FIGURE 2.3.
Close up of Lot 28 from 1718 Stoddart map of Annapolis.

In 1737 Dr. Charles Carroll purchased Lots 25, 26, 28, 29, and 32 from the Garrett heirs. Carroll rented the property to several different tenants. By 1745, Lot 28 was occupied by John Chalmers, who operated it as a bakery complex. A deed entry describes the property as "part of a Lot No. 28 consisting of one Dwelling House Kitchen and Meat House with all that part being the north-ernmost part of the said Lott from the Northernmost corner of the Bakehouse in the occupation of John Chalmers."[2] This reference is the earliest confirmation that the property acted as a colonial bakery. John Chalmers was the baker renting the property, and there may have been as many as four separate struc-tures—dwelling house, kitchen, meat house, and bakehouse.

In 1747 Annapolis was designated an official tobacco inspection site. To-bacco was a major cash crop for the mid-Atlantic colonies of Maryland and Virginia (Middleton [1953] 1984; Kulikoff 1986). Tobacco was a sort of cur-rency as well. An advertisement in the *Maryland Gazette* in 1748 announced goods and services that would be sold for "ready Bills, Tobacco, Current Money, good clean Barley at 3f3 per Bushel, Wheat at 4f, Indian Corn at 2f3, Flour, or Ship Bread."[3] The economic system was predicated on barter and ex-change of goods, and in that system tobacco, as well as baked ship's bread, were mediums of exchange. The development of the tobacco inspection system was meant to ensure the product shipped to Europe was of a high quality and thus keep overseas prices high. Annapolis had been made the political capital of the Maryland colony, and with the addition of the tobacco inspection station the town transformed into a center of economic activities for the region. Chalmers's Bakery was part of this wave of growth in Annapolis in the 1740s.

BAKING IN THE EIGHTEENTH CENTURY

In England, baking was closely regulated, and bakers had to pass a training course before they could practice commercially. The grain trades and baking were considered too important to the general good of the public to be left to the discretion of profit-minded individuals (Middleton 2001). European regulations were carried over to some colonies, including New Amsterdam, Massachusetts, and South Carolina. In New Amsterdam (and later New York) baking schedules and prices were regulated until 1801. Baking in eighteenth century colonial Chesapeake towns was relatively unregulated. The industry was restricted only by the conditions of the work and the social status ascribed to the position. Baking was hot and hard work in colonial Chesapeake towns, especially in the summer. The baker's workday started very early in the morning, and the bakers had to be willing to endure the hardships of the trade. On the big plantations, the arduous task of baking was carried out by trained servants or slaves, usually for the benefit of the many plantation occupants (Crutchfield 1953). Obtaining competent bakers was difficult, and local newspapers such as the *Maryland Gazette* and the *Virginia Gazette* often advertised the need for bakers. Only in colonial Chesapeake's few urban centers, where populations were relatively dense, could baking be conducted as an entrepreneurial business.

The bake houses and other workshops were located in marginal urban spaces, like waterfront warehouses. Additionally, they were usually near other workshops like grain mills and breweries that utilized the same basic raw materials as the bakers (Tunis 1972). They were often considered a nuisance by the public, and their location was regulated for that reason. An act passed in Annapolis in 1695 said:

> for encouragement of all sorts of tradesmen, or men of calling, to come and inhabit the town aforesaid, . . . that when any baker, brewer, tailor, dyer, or any such tradesmen, that, by their trade, may any ways annoy or disquiet the neighbors or inhabitants of the town, it shall and may be lawful for the commissioners and trustees aforesaid, to allot and appoint such tradesmen such a part or parcel of land out of the present town pasture, as to the said commissioners shall seem meet and convenient for the exercise of such a trade, a sufficient distance from the said town as may not be annoyance thereto. (Riley 1887:63)

For bakers, grains and water were their main ingredients, especially for the hard ship's biscuits. For leavened table bread, yeast could be gathered by collecting the froth from a fermenting ale cask (Crutchfield 1953). An early American bakery would have been an open building, perhaps divided into two rooms. The walls would have been lined with kneading trough, kneading boards, and other implements (figure 2.4; also see McCarney 1998; Bridenbaugh 1950; Crutchfield 1953). Brick ovens were usually at waist height, built on a supporting architectural arch that fed up into a chimney (McCarney 1998; Tunis 1972). The actual oven itself would also be arched. Sometimes stones or "fire brick," which were bricks with a high silica content, were used in construction. But red brick was most common, and provided a uniform heat retention. Sometimes a brick oven would be lined with tiles as a baking surface. Because of their construction, and the necessity of their function, baking chimneys and ovens were generally not repaired but instead were completely rebuilt if modifications were necessary (Crutchfield 1953).

Bakery ovens of the eighteenth and early nineteenth centuries were heated in a way that is counterintuitive to modern sensibilities. A fire was built directly in the oven to heat it (Crutchfield 1953; Tunis 1972). Wood was placed near the mouth of the oven to create a proper draft for lighting. Once lit, the burning wood was moved to the center of the oven. When the wood was reduced to coals and white ashes, and the oven was hot, the coals were scraped out of the oven with a large shovel. The burned coals would sometimes be raked into an ash pit compartment below the actual oven. Next, a stick with a coarse wet cloth, or a mop, was used to quickly clean out the surface of the oven. The product to be baked was then placed inside the oven, it was closed, and the products were baked inside by the residual heat.

FIGURE 2.4.
Image of an eighteenth-century bakery by Diderot.

Bakers occupied an interesting social and economic position in relation to urban cultural development. Baking was a journeyman trade, learned through apprenticeships but relatively undistinguished in terms of skill (Bridenbaugh 1950). Baking was never highly profitable. It could only flourish as a business in urban areas with a resident consumer base as well as ships to supply. The bakers themselves often straddled socioeconomic lines, being working craftsmen, selling to a wealthier constituency. They were reliant on local agrarian market networks to provide the raw grains, and the few other tools of their trade. Agriculture was the most common pursuit in the Chesapeake region, and commodities such as wheat and tobacco were brought to the port towns where traders had warehouses and inspectors could check the products. Wheat grains were prone to spoiling and it was generally milled into flour for storage and shipment. Grain prices were set by the international markets, which made wheat flour expensive as a local market product. Grains were the third most popular commodity bought by merchants after meat and alcohol, but account books show baked goods made up less than 0.13 percent of their business, and that small percentage may simply have been products for the merchant's own dinner table (Walsh et al. 1997).

In addition to the hard work, there were social stigmas associated with baking also. Bakers were often resented within their communities. Their bakeshops were in marginal areas because of the odd hours of work as well as the fear of fire. Bakers were accustomed to criticisms, and many of the same criticisms followed baking everywhere, with the two most important being that bakeries were dangerous fire hazards and that bakers engaged in price-fixing. Poorer people always thought the bakers cheated them, and any rise in prices or lack of bread supply was always blamed on the bakers and millers and seldom on the condition or cost of the grain crops (Crutchfield 1953). The following poem was published in 1728 in the *Virginia Gazette*:

> *The Tale of the T___d*
> A Pastry cook once molded up a T___d
> (You may believe me when I give my Word)
> With nice Ingredients of the fragrant kind,
> And *Sugar* of the best, right Double-refin'd.
> He blends them all; for he was fully bent
> Quite to annihilate its Taste, and Scent.
> With Out-Stretched arms, he twirls the Rolling Pin,

And spreads the yielding *Ordure* smooth and thin.
'Twas not to save his Flour but shew his Art,
Of such foul Dough to make a sav'ry Tart.
He beats his Ov'n with Care, and bak'd it well
But still the Crust's offensive to the smell;
The *Cook* was vext to see himself so foil'd,
So works it to a *Dumpling*, which he boyl'd;
Now out it comes, and if it stunk before,
It stinks full twenty times as much, and More.
He breaks fresh *Eggs*, converts it to *Batter*
Works them with *Spoon* about a Wooden Platter,
To true *Consistence*; such as *Cook-Maids* make
At Shrovetide when they toss the pliant Cake
In vain, he twirls the Pan, the more it fries,
The more the noxious, fetid Vapours rise.
Resolv'd to make it still a sav'ry bit,
He takes the *Pan Cake*, rolls it round a *Spit*,
Winds up the *Jack*, and sets it to the Fire,
But roasting rais'd its poisonous Fumes the higher.
Offended much (altho' it was his own,)
At length he throws it, where it should be thrown,
And in a Passion, storming loud, he cry'd,
If neither bak'd, nor boyl'd, nor roast, nor fry'd,
Can thy offensive Hellish Taint reclaim,
Go to the filthy Jake from whence you came.

The Moral
This Tale requires but one short Application,
It fits all Upstart Scoundrels in each Nation,
Minions of Fortune, Wise Men's Jest in *Pow'r*,
Like Weeds on Dunghills, Stinking, Rank, and Sour.
(*Maryland Gazette*, March 11, 1728)

The rhyme is humorous, but it illustrates the general social perceptions of bakers as deceptive and unscrupulous. Bakers kept odd hours, starting their workday very early in the morning. Combined with the arduous manual labor and low pay, bakers were an odd group. They lived at the margins of colonial society—literally and figuratively—and often quit or moved on to new places as they desired or as opportunities arose.

Despite the limitations of baking as a business, the lack of regulation over the trade in the Chesapeake colonies made it an alluring profession to European immigrants. It was a starting place for many immigrants, whether they came to the colonies as indentures or had the means to start their own shop. In the American colonies, many bakers were German (Duclow 1989).

These characteristic factors of colonial baking—public and private production, low socioeconomic status and product value, and an immigrant industry—make the profession a difficult topic for historians to study in a systematic and comparative way.

THE "CHALMERS" BAKERY

A new series of archaeological excavations were undertaken at 99 Main Street in 2003 as part of the preparation and construction of the Annapolis History Center museum. The Maryland Historical Trust's inventory of archaeological sites lists the site as 18AP21. The excavations located and uncovered the northern portion of the bakery building's foundation, along with a well and remnants of a second building (figure 2.5). From the deed references it is known that John Chalmers was the baker there at least by 1745. Consequently, I refer to the structure as the Chalmers Bakery. Excavations had been carried out at 99 Main Street on two previous occasions, but were confined to small and limited areas (Orr 1975; Wright 1959). The excavations begun in 2003 were also limited by modern property boundaries, which cut the bakery in half. However, the fieldwork was able to expand the excavated areas of the site at least tenfold, and excavated across the areas between both previous projects so as to create one contiguous excavation that showed the structural remains, the soil stratigraphy at the site, and the overall site setting. The archaeological features extended to the depth of the original ground surface, prior to the addition of fill, which was three feet below the present surface.

The Chalmers Bakery was probably a mostly wooden structure supported by a continuous above-ground foundation constructed from field stone and brick. It had been built up from the ground surface, instead of recessed into it, and had an oven constructed of cut stone. Three feet north of the bakery foundation wall was a well constructed of dry-laid bricks. The bakery complex was built on the sloping silty ground that forms the shoreline of the bay. At the time it was built it would have been only about two feet above tide level (although Chesapeake sea levels have risen steadily and the precise shoreline

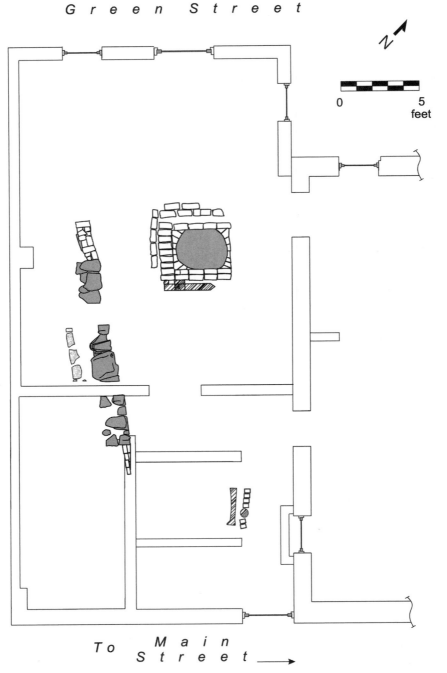

FIGURE 2.5.
Archaeological features of the ca. 1720 Chalmers Bakery, showing their locations inside the 99 Main and 196 Green Street structures.

in the early eighteenth century is unclear). From an archaeologist's perspective, the site was mostly one of archaeological features with little soil stratigraphy of note. There were thirteen architectural elements, which were mainly wall foundations, four portions of floor surfaces, one posthole with the waterlogged wood post still preserved in place, and a handful of other features.

The foundation of the Chalmers Bakery was constructed mostly from large field stones, with brick used to neaten and square the corners. The excavations in 1974 had uncovered the northeastern corner of the structure, revealing a brick corner (Orr 1975). The 2003 excavations began with the goal of relocating that wall, which was immediately encountered on the first day of excavations. That wall was the northern foundation wall of the bakery. Some of the stones in the foundation were as large as two by two feet. The largest were midway along the wall. The bricks were used only to create the corners where the bulky stone walls of the rectangular building met. Where brick was used, the workmanship was a double row of stretcher-laid bricks overtop a row of header-laid bricks on end. The chimney and oven, which were located midway along that wall, were flush with the building's exterior, and extended inside the structure. The interior chimney and oven would have facilitated their use for baking, but it was probably not designed with that kind of functional use in mind. Interior chimneys flush with the exterior walls were a common stylistic technique in Maryland and a product of domestic house patterns from the seventeenth century (Carson et al. 1981; Tunis 1972).

The well was built at the same depth and compass orientation as the bakery building. The well measured 2.8 feet in diameter, but its circumference was not precisely round. Wooden framing was found around the well at the level of the original ground surface, indicating it was constructed through the method known as *steening* or *steining* (Kelso 1984; Noël Hume 1969b). In that process, a circle of wooden slats is formed on the ground surface, and a section of the brick well is built on it above ground. The soil underneath this construction is then dug out until it sinks down. The process is repeated until sufficient access to ground water is achieved. Steening was the preferred method for constructing wells in areas where the water table was high and soils were silty and unconsolidated. The well for the Chalmers Bakery undoubtedly found water at a shallow depth, and is probably not very deep. When excavators located it, the well was covered only by some shallow brick rubble. When this was removed it still had water almost to the top.

Unfortunately, because of engineering constraints and the high water table, the well itself could not be excavated.

The bakery was built up from the ground surface, and construction did not include trenching. This technique of construction precluded the buildup of large deposits of artifacts from the period of construction. Studies of early Annapolis buildings suggest the mixed use of both stone and brick in foundations dated between 1720 and 1740 (Shackel 1994; Yentsch 1994). The earthfast, or post-in-ground, structures of the previous era were sometimes reinforced with the addition of brick or stone around the base, and some early structures were even raised up onto new stone foundations. Archaeological features of the Chalmers Bakery showed no sign of raising, but an adjacent structure on the lot did, with hole set posts that had brick laid between them. The bakery was most likely built on its stone and brick foundation.

The orientation of the bakery and the well is basically true north. This is an unusual alignment for the city of Annapolis where colonial construction was dense and most structures align with the Baroque-style 1695 street plan laid out to complement the topography and the waterfront. Main Street was in its current alignment by 1695 but the adjacent Green Street, which forms the closest intersection, wasn't constructed until 1752. The architectural style suggests the building is from the first decades of the eighteenth century when more permanent architecture using brick and stone was the preference in Annapolis (Carson et al. 1981).

Few artifacts could be securely associated with the construction phase of the bakery, but there is one exception that is notable. Under the largest stone in the foundation wall were large fragments from a North Devon sgraffito slipware bowl with a bright green glaze (figure 2.6).[4] Dates for the manufacture of this ware are 1635–1710 (Miller 2000; Outlaw 2002). The large stone had been placed on top of the bowl, and the exquisite condition of the bowl fragments and its glaze indicate the pieces had been locked in place since the stone was laid. The pottery fragments have sharp broken edges and the fragile green glaze was largely intact when recovered, indicating that it had been sealed in place undisturbed. The combination of architectural and artifactual evidence is intriguing, and the layout of the bakery compound in relation to the city streets adds to that. The bakery structure could potentially have been built prior to the layout of Main Street in 1695. This cannot be verified from the present data alone, and the majority of the evidence suggests a slightly

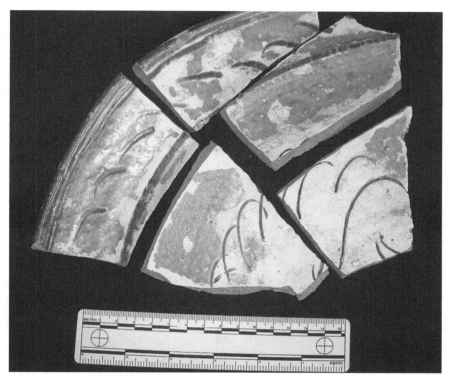

FIGURE 2.6.
North Devon sgraffito bowl. (Photograph by the author.)

later date. Most likely the structure was built in the early eighteenth century, approximately 1720, during Amos Garrett's ownership of the lot and before urban density on the Annapolis waterfront had become an issue.

During excavations, only one side of the bakery could be investigated due to space restrictions. The original Lot 28, as surveyed in 1718, was a relatively large parcel of land. It had been subdivided over time, and as a result the archaeological remains now straddle several properties. Fortunately the half that was excavated was the critical one showing the architectural details of the oven/chimney base. The stones and brick of the foundation wall were "dressed" in a neat line on their northern side, indicating that was the visible exterior of the building. The other portions of the building extended to the southeast, underneath what is now the Bowie Toy Company at 194 Green

Street. The overall length of the exposed north wall was 23.2 feet. The chimney base was built of rectangular sandstone blocks of an orangey yellow color. They were slightly larger than regular bricks, measuring 1.0 by 0.5 feet, with some variation. They were neatly cut stones and were dressed on the southeast, or interior side. The oven extended 2.7 feet into the interior of the structure. Soils around the chimney stones showed clear evidence of thermal alteration, or repeated heating, over a sustained period. Ceramics associated with the chimney stones at the level of the thermally altered soils include tin-glazed earthenwares, brown salt-glazed stoneware (1733–1750), North Devon gravel tempered ware (1675–1760), and redwares, a common mix of ceramics for early eighteenth-century Maryland.

The largest category of artifacts from the site were architectural artifacts (table 2.1), which comprised 33.5 percent of the materials. These included nails, pieces of mortar, and other objects. The next largest category was kitchen materials, comprising almost 23 percent and made up mostly of pottery. Most of these materials date from the time of the bakery's destruction, which is discussed in more detail in the next chapter.

The two previous archaeological investigations at 99 Main Street were both very limited and had reached vastly different interpretations about the site's occupation sequence and dates. Henry Wright's excavations in 1958 suggested the architectural remains originated from the turn of the eighteenth century, while Ron Orr's work in 1974 suggested a mid- to late eighteenth-century date (Orr 1975; Wright 1959). Wright's excavation included one test unit and Orr's

Table 2.1.   Historic artifacts from 99 Main Street Site in Annapolis.

Artifacts Category	Count	%
Architecture	2,320	33.5
Fauna	2,320	33.5
Kitchen	1,580	22.8
Miscellaneous	490	7.1
Flora	71	1.0
Hardware	58	0.8
Personal	44	0.6
Household	30	0.4
Tobacco	18	0.3
Arms	4	0.1
Total	6,935	100.0

two. Both had interesting but very small windows into the material remains of the site—sometimes described as "telephone booth" excavations (Flannery 1976). It is now apparent that Orr's test excavations were focused *inside* the perimeter of the bakery, where artifacts primarily represented the demise of the structure. In contrast Wright's test unit was primarily *outside*. Outside areas were kept neat on a day-to-day basis, but reflect the stratigraphy of major construction changes at the site, including fill layers that sealed the original exterior ground surface.

BAKERY ANALOGIES

Historical descriptions provide some analogies for understanding the construction and layout of the bakery compound on the 99 Main Street property. An advertisement from 1759 for the sale of a Bake House in Alexandria is particularly informative (figure 2.7). While the ad is from Alexandria and not Annapolis, the pattern of settlement style is probably comparable. The advertisement indicates that four structures on a half acre urban property included the following: the Bake-House, a shed with a large oven adjoining, a meathouse, another house of unspecified use that was ten by ten feet, and a stone-lined well. The houses had brick chimneys and were plastered and whitewashed.[5] Urban houselots in the early eighteenth century included numerous buildings. Some housed major activities, while others were minor ancillary structures. From the description in the advertisement it is apparent that bakery complexes in the early-to-middle of the eighteenth century included numerous separate activity buildings, and several dwelling houses. The bakery building might not be the largest, but will have a large oven.

The Chalmers Bakery was also part of an urban compound. The archaeological investigations have yielded relatively good information about the layout of the Chalmers Bakery compound. Little is known, however, about the baker—John Chalmers. There is no census data from the early eighteenth century in Annapolis. Deed books provide some records of the property, but Chalmers was a renter. The fact that he is referenced by name in the deeds is unusual and serendipitous. From his name we have been able to identify a few other activities he was involved in. John Chalmers is known to have employed indentures in his baking business. They would have required dwelling space and may have occupied the tenement on the lot. An advertisement placed by

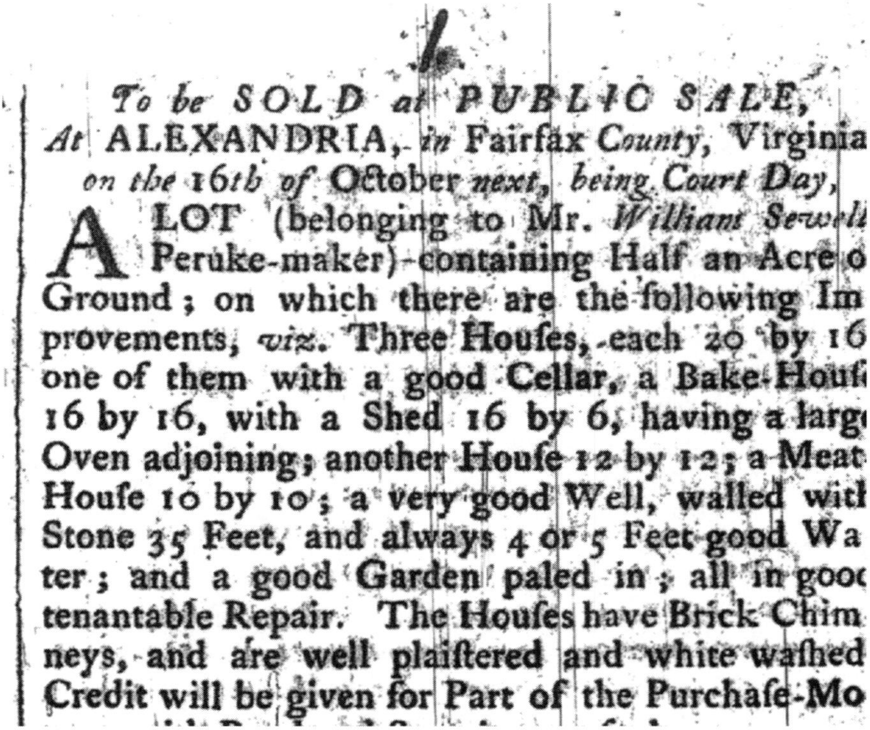

To be SOLD at PUBLIC SALE,
At ALEXANDRIA, in Fairfax County, Virginia
on the 16th of October next, being Court Day,
A LOT (belonging to Mr. *William Sewell*
Peruke-maker) containing Half an Acre o
Ground ; on which there are the following Im
provements, *viz.* Three Houses, each 20 by 16
one of them with a good Cellar, a Bake-Houf
16 by 16, with a Shed 16 by 6, having a larg
Oven adjoining; another Houfe 12 by 12; a Meat
Houfe 10 by 10; a very good Well, walled witl
Stone 35 Feet, and always 4 or 5 Feet good Wa
ter ; and a good Garden paled in ; all in good
tenantable Repair. The Houses have Brick Chim
neys, and are well plaiftered and white wafhed
Credit will be given for Part of the Purchafe-Mo

FIGURE 2.7.
Advertisement for sale of a bakery compound in Alexandria. *Maryland Gazette*, September 13, 1759.

Chalmers for a runaway provides an interesting picture of one of his indentures. He was looking for:

Samuel Coleman, an *Englishman*, a Baker by Trade, a thin Fac'd Man, about 30 Years of Age, a very ugly Fellow; about 5 Foot 9 Inches high, walks something stooping, has a stoppage in his speech, Yellow Complexion, pretty large Nose, very much mark'd with the Small Pox: Had on when he went away, a black Wig, and old Hat, an Osnabrig Shirt, a blue Pea Jacket, a pair of Check Trowsers, and a pair of old Shoes and Stockings.[6]

In addition to indentures, Chalmers occasionally hosted slave sales at his house.[7] Annapolis in the first half of the eighteenth century probably had a population just under one thousand, and it was partially African American (Leone 2005). Annapolis was not a major slave trading town, but as the capital city it was the location for many sales and auctions by residents of the surrounding region. It is unclear whether or not Chalmers's slave auction indicates that he used slaves in his baking business. Slave sales were often held at taverns or other meeting places. Chalmers's house may have simply been the venue for these sales, maybe due to the convenience and proximity of Chalmers's residence to the waterfront docks. If Chalmers used slaves in his business, it is unlikely he could have afforded more than one or two.

PRODUCTION IN THE 1740s

Excavations of the Chalmers Bakery have produced evidence of a typical household craft production system of the early eighteenth century. Chalmers was an artisan craftsman who applied his skills within a small-scale industry. He rented the waterfront baking facilities from Dr. Charles Carroll. The use of space and the physical composition of the baking compound were comparable to similar facilities from the first half of the eighteenth century in other urban Chesapeake areas like Alexandria. There is direct evidence that Chalmers used indentured labor to carry out his business. Indenture labor was motivated by self-interest on the part of both parties, in which the indenture wants to learn the nuances of a craft and the craftsman needs the assistance. There are circumstantial indications that Chalmers may have used enslaved labor as well. Slave labor would have been purchased, but not in a free market sense. The slave had no recourse to demand specific wages or working conditions. In terms of business structure, Chalmers's operation was organized individually and on a small scale. Sales were probably comprised of open accounts to Annapolis residents and merchant ships, paid off through credit or bills of exchange tied to commodities such as tobacco.

Production in the first half of the eighteenth century was very different from that of the second half. At the midpoint of the century the city of Annapolis was undergoing rapid development that continued almost to the end of the century. The Chalmers Bakery represents an early urban production workshop, but it soon became one among many. The increasing commercial base of Annapolis included furniture and cabinet makers, tanning yards, a significant shipbuilding industry with rope walks and ship chandleries, a growing variety of clock and watch makers, silver and goldsmiths, jewelers, portrait painters, and the printing presses for the *Maryland Gazette* newspaper (Brugger 1988; Goodwin and Associates 1993; Letzer and Russo 2003; Middleton [1953] 1984; Papenfuse 1975; Russo 1988). These industries were the result of a growing class of artisan craftsmen in Annapolis supported by a professional and landed group attracted to the colony's political center (Baker 1986).

NOTES

1. Annapolis Deed Book IB 2, folios 29–31.

2. Anne Arundel Deed Book RB 2, folio 197.

3. *Maryland Gazette*, August 10, 1748. Also cited in Mumford (2002:6).

4. Identification of the ware type for this bowl is based on the paste. The base paste matches other North Devon examples in the collections at both the Archaeology in Annapolis laboratory and the Historic St. Mary's City laboratory. The brightness of the green glaze, which differs from other known examples, presumably results from the waterlogged preservation of the piece, and the white slip used for the sgraffito process.

5. *Maryland Gazette*, September 13, 1759.

6. *Maryland Gazette*, October 7, 1747

7. *Maryland Gazette*, February 10, 1747.

3

Fire and the Grammar Bakery

The night of January 21, 1790, the entire lower block of Main Street in Annapolis burned to the ground. The fire occurred in the middle of the night, and historic accounts claim that the Chalmers Bakery at 99 Main Street was the cause (figure 3.1). The bakery had changed hands several times by then, and the baker John Chalmers was long gone. An Annapolis craftsman named Richard Fleming was using the facilities, which were aged and probably in some disrepair. The fire burned the entire block of Main Street east of Green Street, clearing the way for a new era of construction along the waterfront. For archaeologists the fire created a very clear demarcation of before and after, which could be seen in a black layer of sooty soil and burned objects spread across the site. Evidence of the fire was quite apparent in the archaeological excavations. Previous excavations at 77 Main Street, the other end of the block, had found similar evidence of the same fire (Pearson 1991). The current 99 Main Street building was constructed soon thereafter, probably by November 1791.

The demise of the Chalmers Bakery coincided with the period of neomercantilism and changing economic forces in Annapolis. The fire represents a turning point for the economy of Annapolis, and for America as a whole. It was a turning point for urban businesses and especially for the artisan craftsmen. Archival documents suggest the bakery fire was no accident, but instead was an incident of violence within a larger social phenomenon of economic

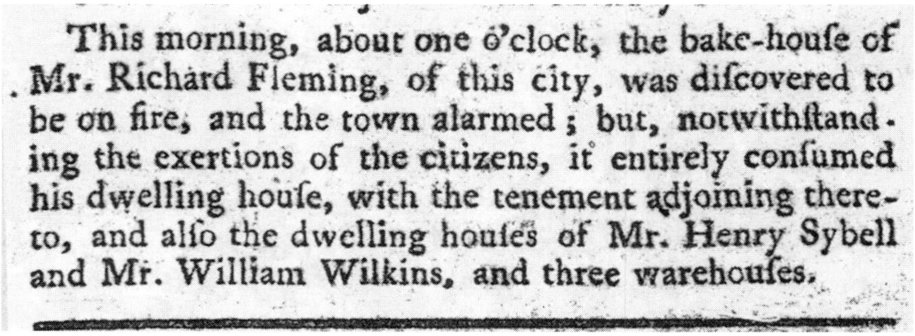

This morning, about one o'clock, the bake-houſe of Mr. Richard Fleming, of this city, was diſcovered to be on fire, and the town alarmed ; but, notwithſtanding the exertions of the citizens, it entirely conſumed his dwelling houſe, with the tenement adjoining thereto, and alſo the dwelling houſes of Mr. Henry Sybell and Mr. William Wilkins, and three warehouſes.

FIGURE 3.1.
Notice of fire at Fleming's Bakery, posted in the *Maryland Gazette*, January 22, 1790.

change and class power struggles. How a bakery fire could suggest malicious intent linked to economic transformation is rooted in the context of the time.

The years 1760 to 1790 were a time when artisan craftsmen in America were free from British restrictions, and manufacturing was not yet dominated by industrialists. In Annapolis, Jonas Green, the printer of the *Maryland Gazette*, flaunted the Stamp Act in 1765 by printing a skull and crossbones where the British tax seal should have been (Leone 2005; Little 1994). The sinking of the *Peggy Stewart* in the Annapolis harbor in 1774 was Annapolis' version of the Boston Tea Party (Schlesinger 1957). Those acts of protest to colonial rule were accompanied by opportunity seekers who sought to position themselves for advantage in the changing system.

Despite public resentment of British rule, merchant activity in Annapolis increased. Between 1763 and 1774 Annapolis experienced a *Golden Age* of construction, spending, and growth. With the end of the French and Indian War, merchant activity in the city accelerated (Papenfuse 1975). With the presence of the governor's court and appointees, the overall increase in wealth, and a preponderance of imported luxury goods, Annapolis emerged as one of the centers of elite style in colonial America (Leone 2005). The process was largely a result of the mercantile economy. Agricultural diversification, increased shipments of wheat, and a growing trade in indentured servants and slaves combined with tobacco profits to encourage the development of a substantial merchant class. By midcentury the port of Annapolis had become increasingly busy. The city recorded annual growth in shipping during the decade before the American Revolution, a large proportion of which involved tobacco (Middleton [1953] 1984). A few merchants could secure a stock of goods from a London firm with bills of exchange drawn on the London merchants or the Bank of England, but most merchants conducted import and export in a symbiotic relationship with the London tobacco merchants. Maryland's exports increased from about thirty million pounds in the 1720s to one hundred million pounds by the 1770s. With this economic development, Annapolis grew rapidly. Fourteen major townhouses were constructed between 1764 and 1774, accompanying luxury gardens increased in number, and construction of a new State House was begun in 1772 (Papenfuse 1975; Ridgely 1841).

It was also the first major era of expansion for production. The idea of political independence was alive, and independence from Britain meant craftsmen would be able to expand their traditional household manufacturing free from regulations. Most didn't wait to see the outcome of the political disputes. In the late 1760s and 1770s urban craft producers began to expand the scale of their production processes. In most American cities, including Boston, New York, Philadelphia, and Baltimore, artisan craftsmen had begun ramping up their operations and organizing trade groups as early as the 1760s. The economy in the 1760s was primarily a market system, based on agricultural production for international sales. The artisan craftsmen maintained localized business for the most part, and they envisioned the expansion of their businesses in terms of making and selling more products. The artisan craftsmen conceived of a scalar growth of their operations, on the premise that increased production would increase profits. It was successful for a short while, but they did not effectively foresee the realignment of manufacturing, finance, and politics that would emerge from the independence movement, and the shift toward manufacturing investments. For the moment, and throughout the war, they were growing.

In contrast to the craftsmen, the wealthy merchant class saw their main stream of revenue suddenly diminish. The European trade market increased but also became more volatile in the period leading up to the Revolution. There were wealthy customers for imported fineries, but the idea of British taxes increasingly rankled colonial port towns. Shiploads of imported goods such as the *Peggy Stewart* were burned by riotous mobs. These sentiments, and the war for independence, presented the most direct problem for those who relied on the import/export industry.

Annapolis thrived during the Revolution, but it was clear that independence would change the makeup of the economic system. The question was how. The wartime spending was good for most of the craftsmen, and at the conclusion of the war Annapolis became the temporary capitol of the new United States for nine months, prolonging the celebration. If America's independence from England would mean less overseas trade and more local manufacturing, however, the merchants would have to insinuate themselves into local market networks and gain control over the manufacturing of the products. Instead of merchants buying, transporting, and selling goods—an exchange system that was based and financed in Britain—it was now necessary for them to buy raw materials, the labor time, and machinery to transform those materials, and also ensure steady sales. A showdown was in place by the late 1780s in Chesapeake towns over who would get which parts of the new economy, and what that new economy would look like.

The conflict of the new economy was brought to a head with the implementation of taxes by the new American government. In 1789 federal tariffs were imposed on many trade crafts. It was the beginning of regulated commerce within the United States. In general, the artisan craftsmen shared the perspective of the Scotsman Adam Smith on free markets. The craftsmen wanted protection from the fledgling U.S. government, and in the terminology of the day that meant they wanted the government to protect free and open trade—ensuring access to markets and shipping with little other meddling in their affairs.

There were many economic problems after the war, but the primary one for the artisan craftsmen was outside of their control. Artisan craftsmen had expanded their businesses within the market economy of the prewar era. In their view, they would produce more volume of product, which would result in more sales. They had trade organizations, and all they needed from the government was "protected" open markets. Those protections were declining by 1790 into government-directed markets. Britain had already developed a manufacturing economy and U.S. politicians like Alexander Hamilton believed that the only way the newly independent country could compete with Britain was with direct federal involvement in economic expansion.

Coincidentally, organized manufacturing societies ended in disaster in New York and Philadelphia. A Philadelphia factory was destroyed by fire in the spring of 1790 under suspicious circumstances (Peskin 2003). In Annapolis, circumstances linking several merchants and bakers culminated in the bakery fire of 1790, changing the lives of many Annapolitans.

THE ANNAPOLIS BAKERY FIRE

In 1773 the *Maryland Gazette* advertised that a baker was wanted in Annapolis "to whom good encouragement would be given," enquire of the printer.[1] A German immigrant named Frederick Grammar heeded that call. He lived on Southeast Street in a one-story frame dwelling house with a brick bakehouse (Letzer and Russo 2003). Grammar was born in Wurttemberg Germany about 1751, and had immigrated to Philadelphia (Papenfuse 1975; Wockek 1999). He arrived in Annapolis in 1777 and was a baker throughout the Revolutionary War, making a small fortune supplying the troops. He is listed in the 1783 tax record as one of two bakers in the city, bringing in a level of occupational wealth equal to cabinetmakers, blacksmiths, surveyors, and tavern keepers (Papenfuse 1975). The other baker in Annapolis was Henry Sybell. The same 1783 tax assessment lists Richard Fleming as a shoemaker, and bringing in a lower income on a level with barbers, tanners, and ship's carpenters (Papenfuse 1975). This cast of characters—Richard Fleming, Frederick Grammar, Henry Sybell, and several others—would all get caught up in the bakery fire incident seven years later.

At the conclusion of the Revolutionary War, Annapolis became the seat of the U.S. legislature from November 1783 to August 1784. It was a festive atmosphere, with the city celebrating independence and hosting dignitaries. Artisan craftsmen continued to find opportunities. A receipt from 1783 shows Frederick Grammar supplied candles to John Shaw, who used them to entertain General George Washington, who was in town to resign his military commission.[2] Another receipt shows payment by the state of Maryland to Richard Fleming, who had sold "95 pairs of men's shoes for the use of the state," presumably shoes for Maryland troops.[3]

The honeymoon didn't last long, however. The easy spending of wartime was over and new economic realities were setting in. The merchant trade business was especially depressed in Annapolis by the 1780s. What remained of the large-scale shipping had moved north to Baltimore, which had a larger and deeper port. The federal legislature moved north to Philadelphia and a depression hit Annapolis from 1785 to 1786. With the loss of the shipping industry, Annapolis' strength lay solely in its role as the state capital of

Maryland. As the town's fortunes declined, so too did the number of landed gentry and merchants within the city. Government officials, tradesmen, shopkeepers and professionals made up the bulk of the city's population.

Within this postwar economic decline, Annapolis changed. The Chalmers Bakery was taken over in the late 1780s by Richard Fleming. Fleming's was the era of urban craftsmen who did many things. He had been a shoemaker during the war, and he held a license to operate an ordinary, similar to a tavern, from the mid-1780s up to 1790 (Letzer and Russo 2003). With this diversity of occupations, Fleming fit the typical social model of a mid-eighteenth-century worker. However, times were changing and he apparently was falling onto hardship. Records from 1785 show Fleming paid Daniel Monroe £20 for "keeping the peace."[4] The perpetrator, Daniel Monroe, was a con man who was eventually arrested. Fleming petitioned the state for a return of his money, pleading that he would have to sell his property below value to support his family. The state agreed Fleming was deceived by the "cunning and misrepresentation" of Daniel Monroe, but only returned him £5.[5]

By late 1789 Richard Fleming had decided to take up baking. In doing so he managed to destroy the Chalmers Bakery, as well as the business of several other Annapolis characters, including Henry Sybell and William Wilkins. The situation presented an opportunity for the Germans, Frederick Grammar and his comrade Lewis Neth, to prosper. Richard Fleming was a tradesman who seemed to be on a steady path of misfortune and economic decline. In contrast, William Wilkins was a local-born merchant living at the south end of the block, at 77 Main Street, and making more money than all of the others. Henry Sybell was a baker and merchant whose house and shop were midblock, basically next door to the Chalmers Bakery. When the fire burned the entire block, Sybell had some momentary hardship. He took out some advertisements in the *Maryland Gazette* that reference the fire at his business, but he recovered. Wilkins presumably built a new warehouse and continued on as before. Fleming did not. Records of the Mayor's Court from January 26, 1790, show that he was assaulted by a man named Benjamin Fairbain approximately the same time as the bakery fire (Riley 1887). The court record of that assault is the last historical documentation of Richard Fleming, and his fate thereafter is a mystery.

Fleming clearly had some enemies, but it also seems that bakery fires of the 1790s were manipulations of the market, perhaps by the merchants but maybe by the craftsmen themselves. The rapid changes from the 1760s to the 1790s saw rapid transformations of the baking business, and also in the economy in general. Merchants saw their business spike before the war, but then suffered considerable loss of business afterward. Many merchants survived on collecting old debts, but they were in need of more permanent solutions to their financial situation.

GRAMMAR'S MERCHANT ALLIANCE

The demise of the Chalmers Bakery under Fleming's watch only seemed to add to Frederick Grammar's ascension of the socioeconomic system. Where Fleming failed, Grammar was the phoenix rising from the ashes. The current structure at 99 Main Street was built by Grammar in 1791 directly overtop the ruins of the burned bakery. The building is a post-Revolution Georgian style brick structure with three stories that encompasses 4,458 square feet. He gave his merchant friend Lewis Neth a ninety-nine-year lease as tenant. In a newspaper ad from 1791, Neth announced that he had moved his business from Fleet Street to the house lately built by Frederick Grammar, opposite the southwest end of the market. Like Grammar, Lewis Neth was also a German immigrant. He is believed to have been a merchant in Europe who arrived in the United States with some capital. He had been operating a store on the dock since at least 1783 (Papenfuse 1975).[6] In the wake of the fire, Grammar had built the 99 Main Street building, and quickly let it out to Neth. Grammar didn't actually purchase the property from the Carrolls until 1792.[7]

The convergence of these various Annapolis characters in the fire incident is uncanny, and is revealing about relations between working-class and merchant-class Annapolitans in the earliest Federal period. By the time of the 1798 Federal Direct Tax records, Grammar was the owner of 99 Main Street, and Neth was the primary tenant. The tax assessment shows the property had a brick dwelling house with three stories (thirty-two by thirty feet), and a brick kitchen (sixteen by fourteen), for a total assessment of $1,000. In addition to Neth's merchant activities, Grammar continued using the facility as a bakery, selling his goods around town. Whether or not Grammar supplied ships with bread is unknown but the diary of William Faris, a clockmaker and silversmith in Annapolis, shows that he bought bread, tea, and brandy from Grammar between 1794 and 1801 (Letzer and Russo 2003:341).

ARCHAEOLOGY OF GRAMMAR'S KITCHEN-BAKERY

The archaeological excavations at 99 Main Street found abundant evidence of Grammar's "brick kitchen" that is described in the tax records, and which he used as a bakery at the end of the eighteenth century. As a reference, I call that period of construction and occupation Grammar's kitchen-bakery. The archaeological work at 99 Main Street was dense urban archaeology (figure 3.2). Because the 1791 structure was built overtop the burned ruins of the earlier bakery, the archaeological site was highly complex, with stratified layers superimposed on top of each other and intrusive features that cut into earlier features. The evidence of Grammar's occupation comes from several strata of soils and artifacts found above the Chalmers Bakery features and the sooty burn line. Most of the architectural features of both the Chalmers and Grammar occupations cross stratigraphic layers. All were sealed in place by a layer of soils and artifacts from the mid-nineteenth century. The Grammar period encompasses the last decade of the eighteenth century and first decade of the

FIGURE 3.2.
Excavations at 99 Main Street showing numerous architectural features. (Photograph by the author.)

nineteenth. Its archaeological signature derives from the building's construction episode, when soils were moved around and leveled, and trenches for walls were dug.

The structure that—at present—has the street address of 196 Green Street is actually Grammar's kitchen-bakery from 1791. This was a lost fact in Annapolis until the archaeological work. The building faces Green Street but, in the manner of urban rowhouses, it is physically connected to the 99 Main building. There have been modifications to all of the nearby structures, making it difficult to interpret age and construction sequence. Historic documents describe the construction of the Green Street row houses in the 1850s and it was believed that they were all built at that time. During the Civil War (1861–1865) Dennis Claude subdivided the 99 Main Street property and in 1871 he gave 196 Green Street to his sister Marion Howes Pinkard to use as a dwelling. It was presumed that Grammar's sixteen by fourteen foot "brick kitchen" was destroyed when the new houses were built. The archaeological and architectural research now show that Grammar's brick kitchen was converted into a single-family dwelling by moving back the rear wall and raising the roof by a story. As such, 196 Green Street is Grammar's 1791 bakery, and the second bakery to be built on that same location on Lot 28.

Excavations beneath 196 Green uncovered the foundation of the former rear (east) wall of the kitchen-bakery structure (figure 3.3). Grammar's original "brick kitchen" had been smaller, only sixteen by fourteen feet. Nevertheless, when Grammar had built it he wanted a lasting and substantial structure. The section of wall is thick and deep, extending down eleven courses of brick to the same original early eighteenth-century ground surface as the former Chalmers Bakery foundation. The style of brickwork was an English wall bond down the center, with an additional layer of brick added to each side. The foundation's construction techniques and dark red brick color matched those of the 99 Main structure. In addition to appearance, analysis of the mortar from the archaeological features and the 99 Main building found that they matched (Sherman 2005). The foundation wall and the 99 Main building were definitely from the same construction sequence. It was superimposed overtop parts of the earlier Chalmers Bakery complex, and many of the archaeological features of the construction intruded into the earlier ones.

When Grammar had built his structures in 1791, the design and placement of his kitchen-bakery was dictated by the location of the Chalmers Bakery

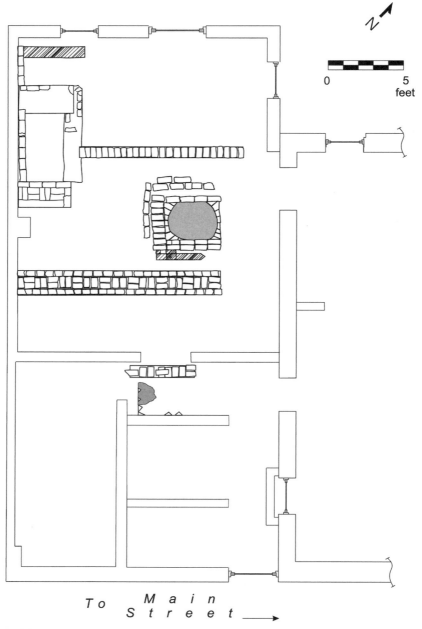

FIGURE 3.3.
Features of Grammar's kitchen-bakery from 1791, showing their locations inside the 99 Main and 196 Green Street structures.

well. Bakeries require a steady supply of water to carry out their operations. The new kitchen building reused the earlier bakery's well, adapting it to the new floor height. The circular well shaft was enclosed around the top by a square brick wall measuring 3.1 feet north to south and 2.5 east to west (to the insides). The east and west walls, the narrower axis, actually overhang parts of the circular well shaft. This well housing was constructed of seven courses of brick above the circular shaft. The first three courses of brick are an orange color, the same as those of the circular brick shaft. The upper four courses of brick are clearly different, and are the dark reddish brown of the 99 Main building. The lower orange bricks are laid in a common English "eight inch wall" bond that alternates headers and stretchers. The dark red bricks comprising the upper four courses are stretcher laid on the east and west walls, and have a few header-laid bricks on the north and south walls in order to fit the spacing.

The kitchen-bakery building is aligned with 99 Main Street. The other row houses that extend up Green Street don't align with the street or the structures, but their two-story height matches. Where the kitchen-bakery abuts the 99 Main Street building it protrudes several feet northwest, making a strange corner. It is now clear that Grammar's kitchen-bakery was built at an odd alignment to accommodate the location of the well. This odd alignment was thought by architectural historians to indicate that the row houses extending up Green Street were all constructed at a later date. It now seems, on the contrary, that the other houses were built to match the alignment of the kitchen-bakery, itself dictated by the location of the Chalmers Bakery well.

Another primary feature from Grammar's building was a large brick hearth. The hearth had been built along the south wall of the kitchen-bakery. Its style was similar to that of a large open fireplace, as seen in other late-eighteenth-century Annapolis kitchens. There was no floor to the chimney but instead two support piers. The hearth was built up from the piers on a supporting arch to put the working area at a comfortable height for the baker. The two hearth piers were each 1.9 feet wide, constructed of the same brick bond as the walls. This hearth, like that of Chalmers Bakery, also extended inside the structure. It was big, with a width of 8.6 feet to the outer sides, 4.8 feet from interior to interior, matching the style found in large colonial homes in Annapolis from the late eighteenth century. The hearth was centered along the wall and had a chimney extending directly upward from it with two flue channels set into the brick wall. During the archaeological excavations the interior of the second floor was removed, exposing the brick wall behind. The marks and patterns on the exposed brick wall, including evidence of the former roofline, provided insight into the structure's original construction and the subsequent modifications. Grammar's kitchen-bakery had been only one story with a pitched roof that probably served as an attic storage space. The two flues extended up from the first floor hearth, indicating the oven had multiple compartments or used two flues to regulate temperature and draft.

A preponderance of creamware pottery (1762–1820) is indicative of Grammar's 1791 construction episode (table 3.1). Soils at the site were largely comprised of deposits from the time the kitchen-bakery was constructed. After the 1790 fire the area was leveled, which created a large layer of soils with artifacts spanning most of the eighteenth century, for the most part dating between the construction of the Chalmers Bakery and the fire. There was some evidence

Table 3.1.   Summary of ceramics from 99 Main Street.

Ceramic Type	Count	%	Date Range
Creamware	189	24.6	1762–1820
White salt-glazed stoneware	81	10.5	1720–1790
Whiteware	81	10.5	1820–present
Redware	72	9.4	—
Pearlware	59	7.7	1780–1840
Tin-glazed earthenware	53	6.9	1600–1800
Slipware	49	6.4	1650–1795
Coarse earthenware	45	5.9	1630–1800
Porcelain	39	5.1	1768–1900
North Devon	14	1.8	1635–1710
Chinese porcelain	13	1.7	~1650–present
Salt-glazed stoneware	13	1.7	1790–1900
Rhenish gray stoneware	12	1.6	1650–1795
Refined earthenware	11	1.4	1600–1802
Refined redware	8	1	—
Hard-paste earthenware	5	0.7	—
Whieldonware	5	0.7	1740–1775
White salt scratch-blue	5	0.7	1744–1775
Yelloware	3	0.4	1830–present
English stoneware	3	0.4	1690–1775
Nottingham	2	0.3	1700–1810
Refined stoneware	2	0.3	~1700–1805
Buckley	1	0.1	1720–1775
Jackfield	1	0.1	1740–1780
Ironstone	1	0.1	1815–present

from the construction of the 1791 kitchen-bakery, but the only clear builder's trench feature from the site came from the hearth base on the southeast side of the hearth (figure 3.4). Ceramics from that builder's trench were mostly from red-bodied earthenwares with gadrooned, or ribbed, sides and a heavy black glaze. The majority have a blistered glaze from being burnt in the fire, an indication that they were remnants of Fleming's bakery operation. These were probably the utilitarian vessels of the baking industry at that time. Other ceramics included pieces of scratch-blue (1744–1775), and white salt-glazed stoneware (1715–1805). Other artifacts from the builders' trench included a couple of gun flints.

Overall there were forty-two features, with thirteen architectural elements and two builder's trenches. Grammar's Bakery had a wooden floor with wide floorboards. The forty-two archaeological features onsite included four intact floor surfaces. Several floorboards were uncovered intact and analysis of wood cell patterning showed they were constructed from yellow or hard pine (McKnight 2005). The composition of ceramics at the site is interesting and

FIGURE 3.4.
Artifacts found adjacent to Grammar's Hearth. Objects in the top row are not burnt, objects in the bottom row are burnt and blistered. All are from the Feature 2 builder's trench, Unit 1. (Photograph by the author.)

suggests a broad array of activities from baking to setting a fine table. Some of the ceramics found at the site may have originated from Henry Sybell's house next door, which was burned in the 1790 fire along with the bakery. In addition to ceramic pottery, numerous tobacco pipe fragments were found. Most were pipe stem pieces with bore diameters measuring 4/64ths or 5/64ths. The calibration of pipe dates by Noël Hume (1969a) for pipe stem bore holes indicates that this diameter of pipe was probably most common from approximately 1710 to 1800.

When Grammar constructed the 99 Main Street structure and the kitchen-bakery, they shared a rear courtyard. It was paved with brick in a herringbone surface pattern. Excavations encountered large portions of this herringbone brick patio. Below the brick patio was a deposit of burnt oyster shells from the manufacture of mortar used in construction. Oyster shells were a common source of lime for mortar in the Chesapeake region. Analysis of the mortar used to construct Grammar's kitchen-bakery, and 99 Main, found it was comprised largely of oyster shell and fine sand (Sherman 2005). Lime mortar from oyster shells does not set properly when temperatures are low, which suggests the construction of 99 Main Street took place in the warm months following the fire, perhaps as soon as the summer of 1790. However, extracting lime from oyster shells involves a process of burning the shells, then slaking or curing them in a pit for at least twelve months to allow them to break down (e.g., Historic St. Mary's City 2004). This would put the date for construction of the house and kitchen-bakery sometime in the spring of 1791 or soon thereafter. The previous excavations of the site by Wright (1959) found a shark's tooth among the shells, which suggests Frederick Grammar may have used oyster shells mined from fossilized beds as a way to accelerate the mortar production process.[8] In the soil profiles of test excavations the edges of the mortar pit formed a pure white stratum while the burn layer from destruction of the earlier building could be seen clearly in a black band below it.

THE LATE-EIGHTEENTH-CENTURY BAKER

Grammar's 1791 structure was designed as a multipurpose waterfront building. The "house" and "kitchen" were really a warehouse and bakery, which also housed various merchant activities. The structures are still standing, although the bakery is somewhat modified. The construction preserved the remains of the earlier bakery below it, leveling the soils across it but reusing the well.

Grammar used his new facilities for baking, but several factors were different from previous bakers like Fleming. Lot 28 had previously contained a multi-purpose compound of numerous structures, each probably no more than one or two stories high. Grammar enclosed much of the lot with a single large structure, the 99 Main building, and an extension off the side, the kitchen-bakery. The design and layout of the buildings reflected the new state of economy and class in Annapolis. Grammar was allied with the merchants, and had built a structure most convenient for mercantile import, trading, and selling.

The bakery off the back side was a small piece of the operation, but unlike earlier generations of bakers he owned the facilities and tools of his trade. His baking business was carried out in a household production setting, but one shared with the wealthy merchant Lewis Neth. The merchant trade was at an all-time low in the 1790s and their arrangement may have been one of mutual convenience. Grammar had a diversity of business interests, as had Chalmers and Fleming. However, the merchant alliance provided financial backing, keeping his capital investments—the buildings—secure. The merchant connections may have also facilitated sales. Unfortunately it is unknown how Grammar used labor in his business, but we can assume it was similar to that of other bakeries of the same time, such as Andrew Jamieson in Alexandria (see chapter 5).

Grammar's activities in the last decade of the eighteenth century, including construction of the 99 Main Street building in 1791, were reactions to a tumultuous economic situation. The previous economy had relied heavily on credit and exchange, as well as the British pound. The credit system was a local adaptation designed to accommodate colonial laws but also facilitate local financial realities. In the 1790s it was unclear what direction an independent U.S. economy would take. Inventive entrepreneurship was central to success.

It has been said that capitalism, to be capitalism, must be capitalism-in-production (Wolf 1982:79). Grammar didn't even own the lot when he built the structures. He had strong ties to merchant capital and goods, which secured his financing. However, there was a level of credit and trust extended to him by the heirs of Charles Carroll, who allowed him to build on, and later buy, the property. Whether or not Grammar was purposefully looking for ways to expand his trade, his creative alliances were critical improvements for the financing of his business and for diversifying his services. It is unclear how Grammar used labor, but he had capitalized his business at least in terms of facilities. He was an owner, having purchased the lot. With Lewis Neth as tenant, the facilities may have brought him rent income, and the merchant alliance allowed him to sell an array of products such as brandy, along with baked goods. These transformations were incremental and inconsequential in the 1790s. The former mode of production, however, had been skilled artisan craftsman operating out of homes or small domestic workshops (e.g., Dawley 1976; Wilentz 1984). Grammar had constructed a facility designed as an investment and dedicated to business operations. These were subtle modifications to the production process, but necessary ones that established the foundations for the emergence of industry in the nineteenth century.

Grammar would go on to make other investments, including the 1807 patent of a 705 acre tract on the Severn River in Anne Arundel County called Grammar's Pleasant Plains.[9] Frederick Grammar died in 1818 (McIntire 1980), and when Grammar's heirs received the 99 Main Street property in 1819, its value, assessed at $1,000 in 1798, had risen to $3,520.

NOTES

1. *Maryland Gazette*, December 16, 1773.

2. Maryland Archives, Scharf Collection 83-11772.

3. Maryland Archives, Scharf Collection 94-14042.

4. Maryland Archives, Scharf Collection 60-7354, 60-7355.

5. Maryland Archives, Scharf Collection 60-7354, 60-7355.

6. From the *Maryland Gazette*, December 4, 1783.

7. Annapolis Deed Book JG 2, folio 611.

8. Anne Arundel County Patent Record IC S, p. 522.

9. Fossilized shell deposits are common along Maryland shores of the Chesapeake, such as the Calvert Cliffs State Park.

4

Money and Markets— The Scots Model

This book describes changes in urban craft production in response to changing economies of the Chesapeake region. Any study of capitalism and its development requires a close look at the monetary system that supported economic transactions. This chapter deviates from the focus on bakeries and production in order to examine the economic transitions taking place in Maryland and Virginia in the late eighteenth century. Hard currency was rare in the colonies. After the Revolutionary War, daily lives of Americans were a struggle for currency—both literally and figuratively. The use of money as currency makes transactions neat. The absence of money required intricate systems of bookkeeping with credits and balances. After the war, the new United States set a goal of developing a banking system, but it took years to conceive, and decades to fully implement. The system that emerged was based largely on the Scottish model of branch banks and credit, which had existed in a sense before the war (Ripley 1893). The towns of Annapolis and Alexandria, as Scottish towns and centers of merchant activity, were instrumental to that process.

With the culmination of the Revolution, the role Annapolis held as a center of economic activities had peaked. Annapolis was eclipsed by Baltimore, to its north, which had deeper harbor access. At the same time, other regions of the Chesapeake such as the Potomac River Valley and the port town of Alexandria experienced growth. Both Annapolis and Alexandria were surrounded by large plantations and were focal points for wealthy gentlemen, politicians, merchants, and craftsmen. In 1790 the U.S. Congress chose the Potomac River as the site for the new national capital city of Washington, D.C. (Bowling 1988), a decision that shifted the center of political and economic activity west from Annapolis. George Washington was the hero of the Revolutionary War and he lived along the Potomac. Washington had presumably influenced the decision over the capital city's location, and there was a belief that Alexandria might become the center of the new federal city.

The context of economic activities in the Chesapeake region was unique. Under the colonial system the British Parliament did not allow export of English coins from the British Isles and had refused to grant permission to establish separate mints overseas except for brief experiments in Virginia in 1642 (Ripley 1893) and Massachusetts in the 1650s (Perkins 1980). An attempt by Cecil Calvert, the second Lord Baltimore, to mint his own coins in England and ship them to his Maryland colony in 1659 lasted only a couple of months (Mumford 2002). Prior to the Revolution colonists relied heavily on silver and gold coins from Spain's New World mines for everyday monetary transactions. Spanish coins were the common specie of the colonial Chesapeake, but even they were relatively rare. Some colonies issued their own paper money in the mid-eighteenth century but those issues steadily and quickly depreciated in value. Acts of the British Parliament of 1751 and 1764 prohibited paper money from being designated legal tender in private transactions in American colonies. Parliament revised the laws in 1773 to permit paper currency issues to be legal tender in public payments, but the ban on private debts remained in force, consequently the system changed little. Foreign coins in America inevitably became overvalued and colonists constantly complained in newspapers and other media of the dearth of specie.

The unpredictable monetary situation forced the American colonies into an elaborate system of compensation notes and credit in lieu of hard currency. It was common to see advertisements in newspapers where goods were being sold "for ready cash, bills of exchange, or merchant notes."[1] Prior to the Revolution, Scottish merchants controlled the tobacco trade in the Chesapeake tidewater region, especially in the Potomac River Valley. The firm of John Glassford & Company opened a chain of stores along the Potomac in the 1750s and 1760s, and was one of the most successful of the Scottish trading houses. They were closely intertwined with economic development in southern Maryland and Virginia. The Scottish merchants readily extended credit to their customers, and their *stores* were the progenitors of modern banks. In the decade preceding the Revolution, the Scottish credit system financed an economic expansion throughout the Chesapeake region that would have been impossible otherwise (Kulikoff 1979, 1986; Soltow 1959).

The rise of the American banking system is closely linked to the rise of commerce in the Potomac River Valley. The following discussion of banking extends back in time to the 1740s but brings the discussion forward to the postwar era of the 1790s. The role of Glassford & Company in the development of the Potomac Valley is discussed, highlighting how the firm was a model for the American financial system. Glassford & Company stores imported and sold many of the material items, such as ceramics, that archaeologists now find on historic sites. The Scottish trading houses provided a forum for most transactions, carefully adapting to the prevailing system of exchange and barter. Nevertheless, some attempts were made in the colonies to mint coinage. One example is the Chalmers Mint in Annapolis. The privately minted coins are an interesting example where the tenuous monetary system resulted in economic experimentation.

JOHN GLASSFORD AND THE SCOTTISH MARKET

In 1772 tobacco accounted for 80 percent of American imports to Scotland, and the three largest firms conducting that trade were Alexander Spiers & Company, William Cunningham & Company, and John Glassford & Company (Kulikoff 1986; Price 1954). These firms had started only a decade or so earlier and succeeded in opening more than sixty large and diversified general stores by extending easy credit to their customers (Kulikoff 1986). By the 1770s the Scottish trading firms had taken over the Chesapeake tobacco trade. Glassford & Company controlled a major portion of the trade, especially along the Potomac River. The man behind the company, John Glassford (1715–1783), became one of the most prominent and prosperous of the Scottish *tobacco lords* (Devine 1990). By the end of the eighteenth century the Scottish model of market finance spread by Glassford and his contemporaries would become the model for the new American banking system.

The Scottish traders were initially drawn to American tobacco as a commodity crop valued in Europe, but they quickly realized there was more profit if they could control the product at its source. Glassford & Company built a series of branch stores along the Potomac that were like trading posts. John Glassford was a student of Adam Smith's and was a clever economist and businessman. Glassford himself never traveled to America, but instead sent young Scots to be his representative agents, or factors. The stores purchased tobacco directly from planters, and in turn sold the planters imported goods. Glassford and his associates were able to pay the growers higher prices for tobacco than English consignment merchants, and provide them with consumer goods at the same time. The Scots had an established system of extending credit to their customers, which was critical in the cash-poor Chesapeake colonies. Debts at the stores did not have to be paid in full for at least four years, and could be balanced out with tobacco notes or other collateral (Kulikoff 1986). It was a business model well fit for the time and place, and the flexible financial arrangements of Glassford & Company brought the firm a large portion of the lucrative Chesapeake tobacco trade. At the same time the individual branch stores sold imported goods such as firearms, cloth, rum, wine, sugar, salt, teas, dyes, paper products, and furniture. Of particular importance to archaeologists, they also sold a wide variety of the *durable* goods that are found on historical sites, including ceramics, glass and crystal, table settings, hardware, and construction tools (Blaszczyk 1984). The local branch stores also served as tobacco checking stations for their respective towns and processed deposits and transfers of cash or notes, similar to a modern bank or notary.

Alexander Henderson was a twenty-year-old Scot when he came to Virginia to work at his brother Archibald's store on the Potomac at Quantico Creek in Dumfries, Virginia (Devine 1990; Hamrick 1999; Mack 1987; Sprouse 1975). In 1758 Alexander opened a new store a little upriver in Colchester, Virginia, where the Occoquan River flows into the Potomac. Within a couple of years Alexander Henderson ran numerous stores along the Potomac, and he has been called the "Father of the Chain Store" (Ward 2001). On March 11, 1767, Henderson bought Lot 31 in Alexandria, now the 200 block of North Lee Street, from Philip Alexander and opened the Alexandria branch of Glassford & Company. In addition to tobacco, the Alexandria branch of Glassford & Company bought substantial quantities of fish for export before the Revolution (Preisser 1977). By the 1790s Alexandria would be the biggest single market on the Potomac, but by that time Glassford & Company had quit the town. After the Revolution and the ensuing economic transformations, Henderson closed shop in Alexandria. focusing on more rural areas. Alexandria was no longer a tobacco town and the branch stores in the smaller towns of Piscataway and Colchester offered less competition and consequently more of the market share. Coincidentally the same Lot 31 in Alexandria would become the Jamieson's steam bakery (see following chapter).

The store records of Glassford & Company are now a wealth of historical information.[2] Given the credit structure, meticulous record-keeping was a necessity of the business. Archaeologists have begun to use the Glassford records in collaboration with discussions of eighteenth-century household material culture and consumer patterns (Furgerson et al. 2005; DeLeuw, Cather, & Co. 1999). The inventory records from Henderson's Glassford & Company store in Piscataway, on the Maryland side of the Potomac, have been used to examine the eighteenth-century market in ceramics in the Potomac Valley, looking at the availability of domestic and imported wares (Blaszczyk 1984).

THE PISCATAWAY STORE

Glassford & Company had a successful business model. John Glassford was not the only Scottish merchant operating on the Potomac, and other noted firms included Dalzell, Oswald, & Company, as well as Hugh Blackburn & Company, and other smaller traders (Devine 1990; Soltow 1959; Sprouse 1975). With Glassford's success, however, he absorbed smaller companies in the western Chesapeake. One of the areas where the Glassford store cornered the trade was Piscataway (Blaszczyk 1984). Piscataway is located on the Maryland side of the Potomac, just downriver from Alexandria. The town was first occupied in the 1600s, and due to a lack of subsequent development in the area, Piscataway has been called "the best preserved, most completely intact, least intruded upon of the old tobacco inspection ports" (Owens 1973).

Piscataway was surveyed and settled in the final quarter of the seventeenth century, and established as an official port town in 1707 (figure 4.1; Kellock 1962). An interesting piece of colonial lore provides insight into the early days of the Piscataway settlement—the year the town was established, Ebenezer Cooke's infamous tale *The Sot-Weed Factor* was published in London (Cooke 1707). The poem describes a would-be tobacco trader who first arrives in America when his boat docks in the cove at "Piscato-way." Cooke's satirical portrayal describes a raucous scene among colonial settlers at the turn of the eighteenth century. The Piscataway area thrived on the Chesapeake tobacco

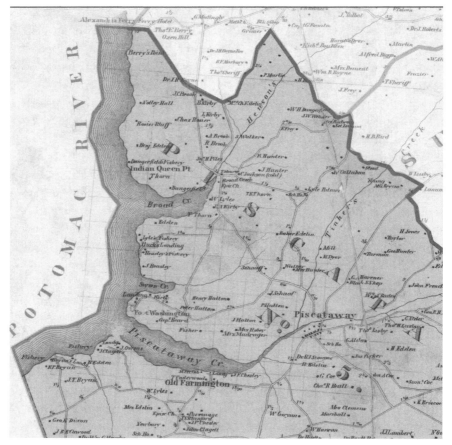

FIGURE 4.1.
Martenet map of Piscataway, District No. 5, in 1861, showing Piscataway Village, on
Piscataway Creek, and the Alexandria Ferry at top left (Martenet 1861).

trade. As part of the Maryland General Assembly's regulation and stabilization
of the tobacco industry, in 1747 the town was selected as the site of a tobacco
inspection warehouse. Piscataway prospered as one of the most important inspection stations in Maryland and developed into a substantial community
prior to the Revolutionary War.

Piscataway initially contained storehouses for several Glasgow trading
firms, but Glassford's store quickly absorbed its competition in the town

(Pearl et al. 1991). The Glassford record books list every tobacco transaction from 1753 to 1844, as well as purchases of goods from the store by local residents (Glassford & Co. n.d.; Papenfuse 1972; Price 1954). While store ledger books are not exciting reads, the local residents of the Potomac were a distinguished and well-known group. George Washington's estate, Mount Vernon, was directly across the Potomac River from Piscataway. Washington had his London agents sail their vessels to Piscataway Creek to be cleared of barnacles while shipments of goods were discussed. George Mason lived at Gunston Hall, slightly south of George Washington on the Virginia side of the Potomac, and was a regular customer of Glassford's Piscataway store.[3]

EDELEN'S MOUNT

The Edelens were a prominent family living in Piscataway and were frequent customers at Glassford's store (Newman 1971). A discussion of excavations at the Edelen residence demonstrates how closely the Glassford stores were linked into the financial and material world of the late-eighteenth-century Chesapeake tidewater area. Excavations in 2003 and 2004 uncovered the remains of several dwelling houses in Piscataway dating from the early eighteenth to early nineteenth centuries. The central and oldest one was known as Edelen's Mount. In 1745 Edward Edelen (1675–1756) willed to his son James (1710–1768) several tracts around Piscataway Village including those named *Thomas His Chance* and *Little Ease* (Furgerson et al. 2005).[4] In 1748 James began to buy up surrounding properties, and he realized his inheritance in 1756 (Fischler [1940] 1999; Newman et al. 1971). The parcel Thomas His Chance was his central residence, and his wife's parents lived next door on part of Littleworth. In 1762 James Edelen applied for an official resurvey of his properties and adjacent vacant lands to the north, and renamed the entire tract Edelen's Enlargement.[5] The archaeological site, with the Maryland state site number 18PR478, is the main residential dwelling that was occupied by James Edelen and his family on the tract.

The property contained an agricultural complex, including the main dwelling just off the top of the knoll facing south, at least five outbuildings, and a well. Excavations at the main house stripped away 2,145 square meters of soil, revealing 157 features, including two cellars and numerous postholes (Furgerson et al. 2005). A total of 12,793 artifacts were recovered during the work, including 98 prehistoric pieces associated with the Piscataway Indians (table 4.1). Of the 157 archaeological features, 88 were postholes (and/or post-mold) features. The many post features and large quantity of brick indicate the dwelling was a post-in-ground structure, possibly with brick piers added. It was finished with wattle and daub, and had one or more brick chimneys. A disturbed brick floor just north of the two cellar holes is interpreted as the remains of an attached kitchen.

The ledger books of yearly purchases from Glassford's Piscataway store provide an interesting set of evidence against which to evaluate the archaeological materials. Glassford & Company ledgers show James Edelen making large purchases in the 1760s, soon after the store was established. These mostly consisted of consumable products like cloth (silk, satin, chintz, Buckram, cotton, wool, etc.), but also boys' fine shoes, jacket buttons, a necklace, blankets, gun screw, cinnamon, nutmeg, 1 box Anderson's Pills (a patent medicine), and bottled drinks including wine, Madeira, claret, rum, and India Passion.[6] These were paid for predominantly with tobacco notes deposited at the Glassford branch stores in Piscataway, Broad Creek, and Port Tobacco.

James Edelen died in March of 1768, and the real estate properties he owned were divided among his sons, Edward, Samuel, James Jr., and Joseph. The family estate, then called Edelen's Enlargement, went to the oldest son Edward (1747–1811) along with some nearby tracts including Little Ease, Hazard, and parts of Littleworth. Outlying lots like Appledore went to James Jr. (1754–1814) or Joseph (1757–833), while Samuel (1752–~1819) received tracts to the south in Charles County, including Friendship and Smallwood's Meadow (Newman [1940] 1971). As the oldest, Edward took over the duties

Table 4.1.   Historic artifacts from the site Edward Edelen's house in Piscataway.

Artifact Category	Count	%
Faunal	4,255	33.5
Kitchen	4,164	32.8
Architecture	3,766	29.7
Miscellaneous	195	1.5
Floral	90	0.7
Activities	87	0.7
Tobacco	71	0.6
Furniture	25	0.2
Clothing	24	0.2
Personal	10	0.1
Arms	8	0.1
Total	12,695	100

of running the family household, and his name appears frequently in the Glassford ledger books after 1768.

The Glassford stores functioned like notaries or banks for their local communities. The Piscataway books record payments for various services in addition to purchases of products. For example, on March 18, 1769, Edward Edelen made a payment to "William Jenkins, Carpenter," at the Glassford & Company store, and on April 4, 1772, he made a similar payment to the sheriff of Prince George's County for services.[7] In 1772, Edward Edelen bought numerous kitchen furnishings, including "1 doz. Cream plates, 1 doz. Knives and forks, 1 Cream Tea Pott, 1 Chaffing Dish, 2 Frying Pans, 1/2 doz. Table Spoons," and other materials.[8] Edelen was fond of creamware, but the store sold many types of ceramic dishes. Specific types of ceramics recovered during the archaeological research at site 18PR478 included the cauliflower Whieldonware, which was known to have been sold at the store (Blaszczyk 1984). Creamware sherds recovered at the site are probably some of the same dishes that Edward Edelen bought in 1772.

By the time of the Revolution, and the census of 1776, the Edelen household consisted of Edward, who was then twenty-nine, his mother Salome, and all of his brothers and sisters. Two other women, Betty Gill aged forty-four and Catherine Curtin aged sixty, were also listed along with twenty-four slaves (Newman 1971). Edelen's Enlargement was an estate in a village setting. With Alexandria to the north, Annapolis to the northeast, and the rapid growth of the surrounding areas, the Edelen household steadily shrunk during the 1780s. Edward remained unmarried, and his seven sisters married into other families. The 1790 census shows Edward maintained the house with two male occupants under sixteen, two female occupants, and thirty slaves. However, changes start to take place in 1795 or soon thereafter.

The records of Glassford's store brought an intriguing parallelism to the excavations at Edelen's residences. Recall that major economic changes were under way regionally in the 1790s. The ledger of 1795 lists the purchases made by Edward Edelen at the store. He was apparently upgrading his parent's old house, and he was also constructing a new house slightly closer to the main road through town. The store records for the year 1795 show Edward buying thousands of pieces of hardware and tools.[9] The Glassford book entry includes several thousand nails and brads, as well as a collection of hinges and chamber door locks. The purchases also include a cooper's adze, chisel, several gimlets, and a dove tail. In addition to hardware and tools, Edelen made a payment at the store for lime, and bought interior furnishings, including an iron pot, a dozen tablespoons, and a few bottles of snuff. These purchases contrast dramatically with those of previous years, which were predominantly cloth and other items of apparel. It is clear from the documentation and archaeological evidence that Edward Edelen was re-creating his estate. The young Glassford factor Alexander Henderson had made similar purchases from Glassford's Colchester, Virginia, store when he had built his house (Sprouse 1975).

The construction activity brought a new house and a new name—Mount Air. A newspaper advertisement in the *Maryland Gazette* from November of 1795 announced that "Mr. Tayloe's horse Grey Diomed will stand to cover mares at Mount Air, near Piscataway (figure 4.2).[10] The area of Prince George's County that includes Piscataway is known for horse racing. Apparently the bachelor Edward Edelen was a planter but also an avid horse racer and breeder as well. Mount Air was the new house Edward had built on a portion of the property, likely for his brother Joseph who had married in 1788 and had several growing children.[11] The name for the new house he borrowed from Tayloe's house, Mount Airy, in Richmond County, Virginia.

In 1797 Edward Edelen had his entire collection of real estate tracts resurveyed and legally renamed Edelen's Mount, an estate of 873.5 acres accumulated from inheritance as well as purchases made over many years.[12] The

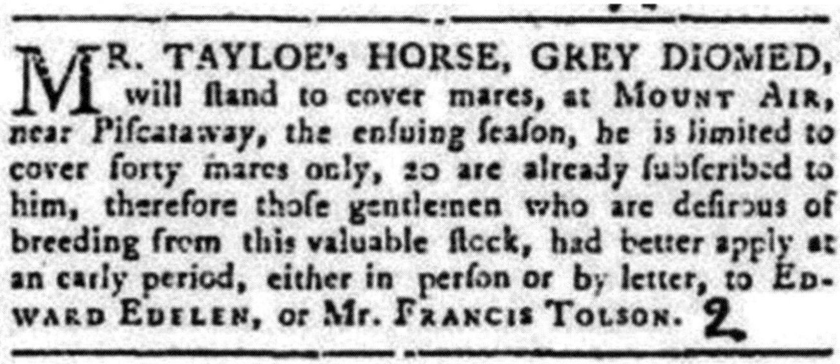

MR. TAYLOE's HORSE, GREY DIOMED, will ſland to cover mares, at MOUNT AIR, near Piſcataway, the enſuing ſeaſon, he is limited to cover forty mares only, 20 are already ſubſcribed to him, therefore thoſe gentlemen who are deſirous of breeding from this valuable ſtock, had better apply at an early period, either in perſon or by letter, to EDWARD EDELEN, or Mr. FRANCIS TOLSON.

FIGURE 4.2.
Advertisement for Tayloe's Horse, Grey Diomed, at Mount Air, posted in the *Maryland Gazette*, November 19, 1795.

resurvey and renaming of the estate coincided with the fact that Edward was then the sole owner. The second house—Mount Air—eventually became known as the Edelen House, while Edward, as the aging bachelor, lived in the residence on the hill that had originally been his parents house.[13] By the following year, and the 1798 Federal Direct Tax, Edward is listed as having one wooden dwelling house sixteen by thirty feet with one kitchen fourteen by twelve feet, all on one acre and appraised at $160. Residential lands were taxed differently from agricultural land, but the one acre actually reflects Edwards reduced holdings. Having built the new house for his brother Joseph's family, Edward passed most of the land to him as well. Joseph was listed in the census with 785 acres. Joseph eventually inherited the entire property after Edward's death in 1811 and Joseph's son Horace owned the property until his death in 1882.

Excavations concentrated at the original Edelen homestead where Edward had lived as a child and an adult. In addition to the eighty-eight posthole features and two cellars, excavations found a well, a disturbed brick floor, one trash midden, and twelve pits that had trash and bricks (Furgerson et al. 2005). A total of 2,564 diagnostic ceramics were recovered, and the ceramic types in the collection concentrated around the middle eighteenth century and the early nineteenth (table 4.2). There is a peak of ceramic dates from approximately 1740 to 1760, reflected in tin-glazed earthenwares, Buckley earthenware, and white salt-glazed stoneware. That was the period when the many Edelen children grew up on the estate. The creamware, pearlware, and whiteware reflect Edward Edelen's continued use of the property toward the end of the century, and some additional use of the house after his death.

The Edelens represent a typical interaction of Chesapeake planters and Scottish merchants in the Market economy. Edward Edelen lived in the old Edelen family dwelling built when Piscataway was growing in the early 1700s. Piscataway was an early settlement that never grew beyond the scale of a village. Glassford's store was central to the Piscataway village life, both before and after the Revolution. Several generations of Edelens lived a comfortable agrarian lifestyle, which was recorded in the sales records of the store. Edward Edelen bought household goods, consumable products, and construction materials from the store. He used the Glassford services to carry out financial transactions with other planters, merchants, and state agents, and probably to manage his proceeds from horse racing and breeding as well. When he upgraded

Table 4.2. Summary of ceramics from Edward Edelen's house.

Ceramic Type	Count	%	Date Range
Tin-glazed earthenware	468	18.3	1600–1800
White salt-glazed stoneware	464	18.1	1720–1790
Whiteware	368	14.4	1820–present
Buckley	350	13.7	1720–1775
Pearlware	285	11.1	1780–1840
Creamware	160	6.2	1762–1820
Slipware	120	4.7	1650–1795
Staffordshire slipware	87	3.4	1650–1795
Rhenish gray stoneware	83	3.2	1650–1795
English brown stoneware	30	1.2	1690–1775
Jackfield	25	1	1740–1780
Staffordshire manganese mottled	24	0.9	1680–1750
American blue and gray stoneware	23	0.9	1790–1900
Whieldonware	21	0.8	1740–1775
Nottingham	19	0.7	1700–1810
Agateware	19	0.7	1740–1775
Ironstone	10	0.4	1815–present
Rhenish brown stoneware	3	0.1	1540–1700
Ralph Shaw	2	0.1	1732–1750
Yellowware	2	0.1	1830–present
Slip-dipped stoneware	1	<0.1	1715–1775

his parents' house, and also built an entirely new house on his property, the material purchases were recorded in Glassford's Piscataway ledgers. Most of the goods and services were paid for by depositing tobacco in the Glassford warehouses each season, an exchange process that worked well in areas dominated by agricultural production.

THE CHALMERS COIN MINT ON CORNHILL STREET

After the Revolution, the economy of urban settings like Annapolis and Alexandria was on a different path from more rural areas like Piscataway, and was much more focused on manufacturing. In Annapolis, a goldsmith named John Chalmers took it upon himself to remedy the monetary situation in the aftermath of the Revolution. His name is ironic, as there is no documentation to show a relationship between John Chalmers the goldsmith and the baker of the same name from an earlier generation. Exhaustive research showed that John Chalmers the goldsmith owned several properties on Cornhill Street in the time during and just after the Revolution.[14] The Chalmers Coin Mint site, a small domestic structure on a narrow street, was excavated in 2003. The coins made there are the first silver coins minted in the United States. The Chalmers coins represent a local solution to the lack of money prior to implementation of a national monetary policy. In addition to the monetary aspect, Chalmers may have been trying to force the hand of the legislature in making Annapolis the national capital.

The history of coins in the United States is generally thought to begin in 1792. That is when Congress passed Alexander Hamilton's Coinage Act establishing the U.S. Mint and authorizing construction of a Mint building in Philadelphia. Chalmers had started minting shilling coins in 1783, with an Annapolis imprint and a declaration of value. In 1782 the rate of six shillings to the dollar had been adopted as the legal ratio in Virginia, while in Maryland and Pennsylvania it was seven shillings six pence (Ripley 1893).

Chalmers was the son of a goldsmith, and was himself a known jeweler and metal smith. He was a captain in the Continental army and was a logistics officer responsible for furnishing food, clothing, and munitions to the army. With the conclusion of the war, the city government established several committees to investigate the possibility that Annapolis could become the national capital. In 1783 Chalmers was appointed to one of those committees (Riley 1887). In that same year he began to mint his own coins that affirmed Maryland's independence from England. Chalmers minted several varieties of shillings, a sixpence, and a threepence (Mumford 2002). One of Chalmers's shilling coins is decorated with thirteen interlocking rings and thirteen stars, to represent the thirteen colonies. The obverse shows "I. Chalmers, Annapolis, 1783."[15]

There was a real need to fill the monetary gap after the war. A federal mint was just an idea, and it would be years before it was commissioned and functioning. Under the Articles of Confederation, each state was authorized to mint their own coins. The states of Massachusetts Connecticut, New Jersey, and Vermont had copper cents made by contract from 1785 to 1787. The first U.S. coin was the "Fugio" cent made under federal contract in 1787. Chalmers was on the very cusp of this process, a fact that was actually recognized in its day. A historical account from 1788 wrote:

Annapolis has the honor of setting up the first mint for small silver coin in the United States. A goldsmith here mints on his own account, but with the sanction of the civil authorities. After the decadency of paper money, what with the general shortage of small coin, it became customary and necessary all over America to cut Spanish dollars into two, four, or more parts and let the pieces pass as currency. This divisional method soon led to a profitable business in the hands of skillful cutters, who contrived to make five quarters, or nine or ten eighths, from a single round dollar, so that everybody soon refused to accept this coin unless by weight or opinion; the perplexity of how to get rid of this cornered currency is an advantage to the goldsmith mentioned, who takes them at a profit in exchange for his own round coin. On the obverse of his shillings and half-shillings stands his name, I. Chalmers, Annapolis; in the middle two hands clasped; on the reverse: One Shilling, 1783; and two doves billing. (Schoepf 2007 [1788])

His accomplishments were unique in the fact that the date was 1783. Annapolis was the national capital for almost a year, from 1783 to 1784, and hosted meetings of the national legislature and other functions during that time. The coins produced by Chalmers are the earliest known coins of an independent United States, and minted in the year that Annapolis was the nation's capital.

Cornhill Street runs downhill from the Maryland statehouse in the center of Annapolis. John Chalmers was believed to have lived in a house near the top of the hill, but he owned other properties on the street. It has been presumed that he rented them out to tenants. Number 10 Cornhill Street is a small brick house on an odd triangular lot at the base of the hill where Cornhill and Fleet Streets converge. Architectural historians had always remarked that for a small house 10 Cornhill had an unusually large chimney (figure 4.3). There was speculation among numismatists that this may have been Chalmers's smelting shop, but the prevailing belief among city historians was that Chalmers lived in the nicer house up the street.

In 2003, the owners of 10 Cornhill undertook renovations to the house. Annapolis resident Will Mumford had published a volume of research on Maryland coins (Mumford 2002). He had researched the Chalmers story and was interested in the 10 Cornhill property. When the renovation plans were announced, including digging out a full basement with a rear stair access, Mumford asked the owners if he could excavate under the house before work started. He had to crawl in on hands and knees through a narrow window and work in a permanently hunched position. After digging through two feet of fill Mumford hit a brick floor—the former basement floor. The house had indeed

FIGURE 4.3.
House on Cornhill Street, showing disproportionately large chimney. (Photograph by the author.)

had a full basement in the past. Digging further through that brick floor, the excavations found a five-inch layer of pure sand, then a layer approximately a foot thick laden with artifacts, which ended on a solid clay floor. Although it looked like only a crawl space, the house had a basement with substantial evidence of past activities. Assisted by the Annapolis city archaeologist, Mumford recovered eight coins and thousands of other artifacts, mainly pottery, in several test units.

Mumford bargained for more time to excavate the site; however, the basement was eventually dug out mechanically by construction contractors. The soil from the basement was transported to a safe area where it could be screened for artifacts. Mumford and teams of volunteers screened through the soil for artifacts. One of Chalmers's silver threepence coins was recovered with the 1783 date clearly legible (figure 4.4). Only a few examples of these coins are known to exist (Mumford 2002). Other artifacts from the site included molten drips of metal, slag iron, shaped stone pieces that are probably drying molds for molten metals, and many other coins. Several narrow curved lead objects might be patterns for casting brass (e.g., Noël Hume 1970). A single Spanish bit was also found (figure 4.5). It is an eighth-sized piece from the

FIGURE 4.4.
Chalmers's 1783 silver three-pence coin. Obverse (left) has "1783" at top right, and reverse (right) has "I. Chalmers" across top. (Photographs by the author.)

rule of Charles III, who held the Spanish throne from 1760 to 1788. I participated in several sessions of screening through the pile of dirt that had been
scooped out of the 10 Cornhill Street basement, and personally found four
coins. Two of those were Irish half pennies. The other two were unidentifiable
copper alloy coins.

Overall, thirty-three coins were recovered from the site. Most could be
identified (table 4.3), but a few could not. There were several other round objects recovered that could also be coins, but they are too worn and corroded
to be sure. In addition to the coins, over thirty pounds of iron objects were recovered (Mumford 2005). Most were nails, but there were also several large
keys, pieces of hardware, and tools including a chisel. There were three iron
balls that could have been cannon shot or weights, and many large and small
pieces of slag from both the fireplace area and on the floor. Some were iron
and some not. Melted glass was found in drop shapes, and there were over a
hundred buttons made from bone, oyster shell, glass, pewter, bronze, copper,

FIGURE 4.5.
A Spanish bit found in the basement of 10 Cornhill, from the reign of Charles
III (1760–1788). Obverse (left) shows the VNUM and crown and staff, and re-
verse (right) shows the III from "Charles III." (Photographs by the author.)

Table 4.3. Coins recovered from the Cornhill Street Mint in Annapolis. Based on Mumford (2005) and personal communication.

Denomination	Issue	Date	Quantity
British half pennies	William III	1698	1
	George I	1721	1
	George II	—	5
	George III	—	7
	Unidentified ½ pennies	—	5
British farthing	George III	—	1
Irish half penny	George III	—	3
Virginia half pennies	—	1773	2
Connecticut cent	—	1785	1
Nova Constellatio cent	—	1783	1
Portugal 10 reis	—	1752	1
U.S. large cent	—	1838	1

silver, and one gold plated. Additional personal items include a ring setting, several shoe buckles, a belt buckle, and two sets of cufflinks. A number of gunflints and some raw flint nodules suggest possible gunsmith activities. Thousands of ceramic sherds were recovered, with an unusually high proportion of the combed style of Staffordshire slipware (e.g., Noël Hume 1969a).

I inspected the basement of the 10 Cornhill house after the excavations, hoping to examine the fireplace. The house had an interior chimney and in the basement it formed an enclosed furnace. It had a central portal that opened into a large chamber, and two flues going off in two directions that could each be damped if desired. This large basement furnace indicated that the house at 10 Cornhill Street clearly engaged in activities beyond the average residential household. The chimney for the small, two-story house was so large because it contained four ducts, two extending from the basement furnace and one from each living floor. It seems very likely that this was a late eighteenth-century manufacturing furnace.

The excavation of the 10 Cornhill Street site was conducted under constraints of time and private property. Interpretations of the archaeological data are limited, and there is no full catalogue of artifacts recovered. Nevertheless, the evidence of metallurgical production and the large number of coins is atypical of domestic archaeology in the city. Combined with the design of the chimney, the evidence is more than uncanny, and strongly suggests the location was indeed Chalmers's workshop. John Chalmers probably used this site in the eighteenth century as his metal workshop, smelting down whatever metals he could find, even copper alloy coins, to make objects like buckles for belts and shoes. The silver he also smelted down, and used it to mint coins. The house at 10 Cornhill is the most likely place for those activities. Sometime in the late eighteenth century, the basement workshop had been filled in.

The minting of coins by Chalmers has numerous implications. In 1783 the U.S. legislature had not yet decided where the federal capital city would be placed. Annapolis was made the capital for a short time during that year, and it was a celebratory year for Annapolis in many respects. George Washington came to Annapolis to resign his military command, a symbolic gesture meant to show that the military would play a secondary role in democracy. Washington was highly revered in Annapolis, coming off his war success, and during the legislative session he was shown the best the town had to offer. Chalmers's coins had a monetary value, and were used as such. But he may have minted the coins partly for the symbolism, to commemorate that year and to show that Annapolis could sustain a larger national status.

The Schoepf quote says Chalmers had "the sanction of civil authorities" to mint his coins, but it is unclear what authority he had, if any. Chalmers's actions reflect the desire of Americans to be free of the British monetary restrictions. The coins Chalmers minted were small currency and few in number, but the restrictions they flaunted included large-scale taxes and prohibitions that the colonists had always disliked. With the Revolution complete, Chalmers wanted economic independence, as did many other Americans, a situation that would require a stronger economy based on a new monetary system.

AMERICAN BANKING AND ECONOMIC GROWTH

The decade after the Revolution was one of great change for the former colonies. In 1789, Alexandria and a portion of Fairfax County were ceded by the state of Virginia to become a component of the newly created ten-square-mile District of Columbia. The first cornerstone of the District was laid at Jones Point, on the south side of Alexandria, on April 15, 1791. But the territory was not formally accepted by the U.S. Congress until 1801. Everything was in flux in the 1790s from the currency to the political and economic policies.

The Scottish bankers and merchants had used innovative managerial skills in the late colonial period to build their share in the Chesapeake economy and

John Glassford, following from the Glasgow economic school of Adam Smith, used these concepts to great advantage in his merchant endeavors in the colonies. Not only did the Scots outbid the London consignments on tobacco prices, they created new ways to provide goods and services to American colonists (Blaszczyk 1984). From a modern perspective, the operations of Glassford & Company in the late eighteenth century blurred the lines of a merchandise outlet and a financial institution. The stores were depositories where people could pay county levies and militia fees, trade bills of exchange, and conduct many other types of financial transactions (Sprouse 1975). The Glassford stores even hosted lotteries to raise money for local community initiatives. The stores also engaged in general sales of dry goods, and at the end of the year tallies of daily transactions were transferred to journals and expressed as debits and credits, and posted in a ledger (Soltow 1959). These were then applied to the following year's transactions. Unlike modern retail stores, Glassford & Company acted as a nexus of the community's barter economy. They served as the financial record keepers for different types of public and private activities and also as the local representatives of the trans-Atlantic markets (Blaszczyk 1984; Henretta 1998).

The Scottish capital that came with the merchant industry was partially responsible for the rapid growth of Chesapeake towns in the third quarter of the eighteenth century. The part of that equation that included credit, however, was the most important. The extension of easy credit allowed for local reinvestments of resources in the means of production (Kulikoff 1986; Soltow 1959). The credit system was a creative financing tool, meant to be a service to farmers and planters that facilitated overseas trade. The credit system provided farmers and planters with goods, on the expectation that they would settle their accounts at the end of the crop year. The system was heavily abused, and many debts were simply carried over from year to year. By the outbreak of the Revolution, the combined Glasgow merchant firms operating in the Chesapeake area were owed more than one million pounds sterling from the colonists, much of which would never be realized (Price 1954). Additionally, the economy of the eastern United States, once exclusively agrarian, had an increasing urban production sector with different requirements and constraints on capital than seasonal farming.

There was a lapse of time between the political independence brought by the American Revolution and when the instruments of an American cash economy developed. The minting by John Chalmers of silver shilling and pence coins with an Annapolis imprint is one example in which an individual artisan craftsmen took the opportunity to expand his social roles. Chalmers addressed the need for coinage, and his gesture was timed so as to demonstrate those needs to national politicians in Annapolis.

While Chalmers took initiative, his methods derived from the mentality among many artisan craftsmen that the defeat of British restrictions meant all production could simply increase in scale. On the contrary, the larger economic context was more complex, and would result in a major restructuring of the relationship between manufacturing, money, and markets. Similarly, the development of a U.S. monetary system was more than simply the production of individual coins, and needed to serve an export oriented trade. The new U.S. economy required a formal and systematic plan with institutionalized processes, notes, interest, and paper money. The model for such a financial system was already in use in the Chesapeake tidewater area in the form of the Glasgow merchants like Glassford & Company. The Piscataway store was a particularly successful example, continuing in operation until 1822.

The Scots model of business finance took hold in the Potomac Valley and throughout the Chesapeake, and its tenets became the national banking system expanded upon by Hamilton and others (Coulter 1944; Ripley 1893). Branch banking was a distinctive feature of the Scottish monetary system (Baker 1899), and Glassford's stores had established a method by which local capital could be centralized into a community-based institution with numerous separate branches. City and state banking in Virginia and Maryland expanded exponentially in the first decades of the nineteenth century. In that emerging market in money, individual communities were required to generate the capital to establish a bank. The city of Alexandria led the way in the Potomac region, tapping its merchant wealth and productive base. The 1792 petition to the Virginia state legislature reads:

> The petition of the Merchants and other Inhabitants of Alexandria and its vicinity humbly sheweth: that the experience of commercial Nations for several ages has fully evinced that well regulated Banks are highly useful to Society by promoting punctuality in the performance of Contracts, increasing the medium of Trade, facilitating payment of Taxes, preventing the exportation of Specie, furnishing for it a safe deposit, and by discount, rendering easy and expeditious the anticipation of funds on reasonable Interest. To participate of

these advantages, your Petitioners are desirous of Establishing a Bank in the Town of Alexandria, the Capital of which not to exceed 100,000 Dollars each—Your Petitioners beg leave, humbly to represent, that the Establishment of a Bank in the Town of Alexandria, has become the most necessary, not only to increase the commerce of this place, and of course of the State, but to preserve that share of it which it at present possesses, in consequence of Banks being Established at Baltimore & Philadelphia, through the medium of which the commerce of these Towns are so much facilitated. (Merchants of Alexandria 1923)

Bank shares were sold in Alexandria at $200 each to raise the necessary capital wealth. The Bank of Alexandria stayed true to its roots and the Scottish system of credit, only requiring payment of $10 specie for each $200 share. This early system resembled the Scottish banking system, with a large capitalization, a large mother bank, and many branches, along with the continuation of easy credit. The transition was timely and not coincidental. The new monetary system with new financial controls was implemented in the 1790s, opening the way for systemic change from a mostly barter economy to a capitalistic one. By 1797 Alexandria had become the single most important market on the Potomac, a phenomenon based largely on production facilities and other services within the city, and not simply on imports and sales. Scottish merchants kept stores in profitable Chesapeake towns. They lost the economic dominance they had controlled prior to the War, but their credit system of finance had allowed for investments in urban production that took on a life of its own.

NOTES

1. From the *Virginia Gazette*, November 29, 1770.

2. The majority of the records for the Glassford stores are available at the Library of Congress microfilm room, and can be obtained on interlibrary loan. Records for the city of Alexandria, including Alexander Henderson's (1999) ledger for the city, are on microfilm at the Alexandria Library Special Collections. Georgetown University Library Special Collections holds the papers of Robert Fergusson, Glassford's tobacco factor operating in Port Tobacco, Maryland (Fergusson n.d.).

3. For example, see the entry for August 5th, 1767, R9, C25—in John Glassford & Co., n.d.

4. Most tracts in Prince George's County, Maryland were patented between 1660 and 1690 by frontiersmen expanding the limits of tobacco agriculture. A land patent was the legal description of the land, analogous to a modern deed. The original names for the tracts often indicate the first impression of the land's potential for quick tobacco profits, such as "Little Worth" (see Kellock 1962). The names changed over the years as tracts were bought and sold, and as settlement in the region changed from speculative farms owned by absentee landlords into more permanent family estates and plantations.

5. Prince George's County Circuit Court Patent Certificate 728.

6. See John Glassford & Co., n.d., reel 8, page 62 from 1766.

7. See John Glassford & Co., n.d., reel 15, page 186.

8. See John Glassford & Co., n.d., reel 15, page 186.

9. See John Glassford & Co., n.d., reel 19, page 616.

10. Edward and Joseph Edelen were contemporaries with, and acquaintances of, John Tayloe III (1771–1828), the wealthiest man in Virginia in the late eighteenth century. Tayloe's primary residence was a distinctive stone mansion named Mount Airy, along the Rappahannock River in Richmond County, Virginia. Tayloe was an avid lover of horses, and he raced and bred them throughout Maryland and Virginia.

11. Prince George's County Circuit Court Patent Certificate 732.

12. Associating the house name Mount Air with the existing Edelen House came from the documentation on James Edelen and his children. Mount Air seems to be the name used in the earlier part of the nineteenth century. As an example, in 1817 Salome Caroline Edelen (1789–1819), daughter of Joseph Edelen, married William Eilbeck Mason (1788–1820), the son of Virginia statesman George Mason. The marriage records state that they were married at Mount Air. She died in 1819 and he died in 1820, and the death records indicate both were interred in Mount Air Cemetery.

13. This house was transformed into a prominent brick manor house in the early nineteenth century by Joseph Edelen as his wealth and inheritance grew. It is now called the Edelen House, and is listed in the Maryland Inventory of Historic Properties (MIHP). It is designated an historic site (PG84-23-6) under the Historic Sites and District Plan in Prince George's County.

14. Documentary sources available included a property history for every lot on the street from the seventeenth century to the present, compiled through years of research in the Hall of Records by retired U.S. Marine Corps Colonel Richard Smith who currently lives near the top of the street.

15. The "I" is believed to be a modified "J." See Mumford (2002).

5.

Alexandria and the Mechanization of Baking

The city of Alexandria is similar to Annapolis in many ways as an urban settlement within the Chesapeake tidewater area. Alexandria was at the center of the Potomac Valley economic system. The changing economic forces described for Annapolis in the 1790s were at work in Alexandria too, and perhaps more so. During the war, Alexandria had lost trade. The economy of Alexandria, however, was always more diversified than that of Annapolis. Alexandria regained more of its trading business after the war, but also saw more emphasis on manufacturing.

In the early eighteenth century, Alexandria was the primary destination for agrarian crops grown in northern Virginia. Like Annapolis, tobacco was the initial cash crop, but Alexandria quickly diversified and became a center for grain industries. By midcentury, wheat was transported from western counties like Loudoun to Alexandria to be processed and sold overseas. There were numerous breweries in town (Walker and Dennee 1994), but there were even more bakeries and baking is considered one of the town's main eighteenth-century businesses (Miller 1998). Before the war, the prime trading partner was Great Britain. When the English Parliament imposed sugar and stamp taxes on the Virginia colony, trade relations between the two became strained (Barr et al. 1994). When the English closed Boston Harbor in 1774, disgruntled Alexandria residents passed a resolution calling on all the colonies to terminate trade with the mother country.

The extensive Revolutionary history in Virginia and Maryland is well-known. During that time, Alexandria's many merchants were busy developing the city's waterfront to reconfigure the shipping trade. The Alexandria waterfront was an active port hosting sailing brigs and schooners laden with commodities from the ports of Glasgow, Whitehaven, or London, as well as the West Indies. The ships deposited their cargoes at one of the many wharves, such as Thompson's, or Wilson & Herbert's wharf, where one could purchase broadcloths from Amsterdam, liquors from Cadiz, German and French linens, silver, hardware of all varieties, musical instruments and fancy goods. The old Potomac River tobacco towns like Piscataway and Dumfries, which were heavily reliant on tobacco alone, lost their prominence as the trade became too unpredictable (Duffy 1965). Above all other towns on the Potomac, Alexandria emerged as the manufacturing and export center of the region.

From 1780 to 1820, there were over sixty-three bakers who advertised in the *Alexandria Gazette* or offered their services to the public (table 5.1; Miller 1991, 1992b). In 1796 Alexandria was the seventh largest port in the United States and the third largest exporter of flour. It was an ideal location for bakers, but this led to competition. By the time of the 1834 *Alexandria City Directory*, only fourteen bakers were in business, reflecting the rapid consolidation of baking as an industry. The shrinking numbers tell only part

Table 5.1.   Alexandria bakers, 1780–1820. Based on Miller (1998).

James Adam	James Gullat	William Reed
Ignatius Allen	Searchy Harris	Anthony Rhodes
John Anderson	David Henderson	Benjamin Ricketts
Robert Anderson	Harry James	Lewis Seffley
Samuel Baggett	Andrew Jamieson	Wm. Stacie
Jacob Butts	John Jamieson	Michael Steiber
Thomas Conway	Kinninmond & Oswald	Lawrence Swann
Samuel Cooper	Frederick Koones	John Tatspaugh
Alexander Couper	John Korn	Peter Tatspaugh
Samuel Crandell	Korn & Weismuller	Wm. Taylor
Thomas Crandell	Edward Lee	Joseph Thomas
John Cranston	John Lemoine	John Thompson
George Dagen	Wm. Lovell	Joseph Thornton
Henry B. Dagen	F. McClellan	Henry Walker
John Dixon	James MacDonald	Barbara Wilkes
Andrew Duman	James McFadon	Peter Wilkes
Charles Duncan	Daniel McLean	Frederick Wood
Wm. Easton	William Mills	John Young
Henry Gardner	Wm. Ownbread	Nicholas Young

of the story. The changing environment of Alexandria's baking industry in the first half of the nineteenth century really centers on shifting American perceptions on the use of manual labor, the increased technological developments of machinery to aid production, and the larger reshaping of the economy from one of market exchange to cash-based capitalism.

Alexandria in the early nineteenth century was populated by a talented and diverse group of artisan craftsmen who supplied the local population, as well as the back country, with many goods and services. Many were European immigrants or first generation Virginians, and some were African American, both enslaved and free. In addition to bakers, other trades and occupations throughout the town included blacksmiths, butchers, hatters, house carpenters, music teachers, cabinet makers, coopers, ropemakers, silversmiths, tanners, tobacconists, weavers, and wheelwrights (Miller 1991, 1992b). As in Annapolis, artisan craftsmen in Alexandria were also redefining their positions within a rapidly changing economy, a story that, in this case, *started* with a bakery fire.

Extensive archaeological remains of a steam-powered bakery complex were uncovered by researchers on the 200 block of North Lee Street in Alexandria. The archaeological remains were extensive and included a large cistern, three brick-lined wells, a row of four ovens, and the brick and stone foundation remains of the bakery's four structures. The archaeology and historical research build an insightful narrative of how the Jamiesons expanded baking from household level production into a mechanized industry. The steam bakery complex was built by Robert Jamieson in 1832, but the history of it starts with his father, and with another fire, and adds considerable context to the archaeological remains and the interim period between artisan craftsmen and large factories.

ANDREW JAMIESON & SON

Baking in the early nineteenth century was very different from what it had been only a decade or two prior. We know little about Frederick Grammar's business and community relations in Annapolis, but we can assume it was probably similar to what was taking place with his contemporary Andrew Jamieson in Alexandria. Andrew Jamieson (1749–1823) had been born in Scotland. He established a bakery in Alexandria at Water and Oronoco Streets by at least 1785. Jamieson was involved in an assortment of economic and entrepreneurial activities. In addition to the baking business, he dabbled in merchant trade, having several trading partnerships in the late eighteenth and early nineteenth centuries (Miller 1991). In 1791 he leased Lot 85 at Wolfe and Union Streets, "to repair bakehouse and ovens, costs to be deducted from rent" (Ring and Pippenger 1995:75; Tallichet 1986). Andrew married Mary Sweet in 1794 (Pippenger 2001), and their son Robert (1795–1862) was born soon thereafter. In 1795 Andrew Jamieson bought Lot 4, at Oronoco and Water Streets "with the bakehouse, other buildings and improvements, and use and benefit of the water" (Ring and Pippenger 1995:5).

Jamieson was part of a close group of individuals living on the waterfront who created a lively social dynamic in early nineteenth-century Alexandria. The group included Jamieson, as well as real estate speculator William Wilson, and tailors John Potts and George K. Wise, whose stories are all closely linked. These men and their neighbors can be called the northern waterfront merchants and craftsmen. They all resided around Water and Oronoco Streets (Cuddy et al. 2006). Most were Presbyterians, and many were Scottish.

Jamieson's bakery on the northeast corner of Oronoco and Water Streets caught fire in 1795. The newspaper description of the incident reported that:

> The bakehouse of Mr. Andrew Jamieson caught fire last Thursday morning. Notwithstanding that every exertion was made to arrest the progress of the devouring element, it soon laid waste this house and dwelling adjoining; while the most unremitting efforts of the citizens did with difficulty prevent it communicating to the buildings adjacent. By this unfortunate affair Mr. Jamieson lost a large quantity of flour and bread; the books, papers, and the most valuable of the furniture were removed before the dwelling took fire. (*Columbia Mirror and Alexandria Gazette*, June 27, 1795)

The fire at Jamieson's bakery was probably set intentionally, as suggested for the bakery of Richard Fleming in Annapolis. The public perception that bakeries were dangerous fire hazards was common, but the fire at Jamieson's bakery appears suspicious for several reasons. The fact that valuable furniture could be safely removed suggests the fire fits into the context of other fires with suspicious circumstances in the 1790s. The newspaper announcements of the fires are essentially standardized. They give few details and take no side in assigning fault, simply pointing out how, "notwithstanding the exertions of the local citizens," the bakery burned down. It seems more than just coincidence that these suspicious fires took place at a major point of transition for the baking profession.

The flour industry in Alexandria, on which all the bakers relied, was large and powerful, and Jamieson was occasionally at odds with them. In June of 1787 he had published a public accusation of the miller Robert Adam in the newspaper. Apparently Jamieson had sent Adam a load of wheat to grind, and it came back short. Jamieson challenged Adam in the newspaper, writing, "I am not the first that has suffered the venom of your tongue, and I solemnly defy you and all mankind to prove me guilty of fraud and lies, and I am conscious I do not deserve the base names of villain and cheat from you or any man."[1] In October of that year Jamieson signed with eighty other craftsmen and merchants a General Assembly petition asking for more stringent enforcement of the wheat inspection laws. The petition complained that the quality of wheat shipped from Alexandria was inferior to that of Philadelphia and Baltimore (Merchants of Alexandria 1922). Five months after the bakery fire, on November 12, 1795, Jamieson signed an act compelling millers to brand "superfine" on each barrel of flour judged to be of that quality (Pippenger 1995). It was only the following year, 1796, that Alexandria's City Council began passing acts to regulate the size of bread sold in the city market. The act passed by the Council stated that the

> Mayor and Commonality of the said town shall from time to time have full power and authority to regulatte [sic] the assize or weight of bread whicch [sic] regulation shall be entered upon the minutes of the common council, and the several persons baking bread for sale shall govern themselves to any regulations so made, until the same be altered, and, any person so baking bread shall have any for sale within the limits of the town, under the weight directed by the regulation in force at that time, all bread so for sale be seized by the clerk of the market, or any other city officer, and applied to the use of the poor admitted to the poor house of the said town.
>
> Be it further enacted, That the clerk of the market once in each week examine the weight of bread baked by the different persons for sale within the limits of the town, and compare the same with the regulation of the common council then in force, and when it shall so happen that the price of flour is frequentlty [sic] and considerably varying, that he do on such occasions apply to three purchasers of flour in the said town, as such variations take place, for the best information with respect to the price and obtain from them a certificate thereof

[sic] and publish the same and the weight which bread ought to be of con-
forming to the regulations of the common council, in the Alexandria Gazette.
. . . In testimony whereof I have hereunto set my hand and affixed the seal of the
corporation, this 6th day of Feb. 1796.
—John Dundas, Mayor
(*Columbia Mirror & Alexandria Gazette*, February 9, 1796)

The act was the beginning of tighter regulations in the Alexandria baking
industry. A similar act had been passed in New Amsterdam early in the seventeenth century, but bakers in Virginia and Maryland had enjoyed a relatively
unregulated craft. Many variables of the baking business, and craft production
in general, were changing in the last years of the eighteenth century. The city
only began to regulate sizes and cost because they wanted to purchase bread
products for the orphan's house, but the timing coincided with the overall
transformation of the trade. In addition to the political regulations imposed
by the city, the size of bakery operations, their organization of production,
and their financing were all in flux, but generally growing. There is only circumstantial evidence indicating arson in Jamieson's 1795 fire, but there were
deep motives, as with the Annapolis case, for merchants and other groups to
hold grudges against Andrew Jamieson and his baking business.

Jamieson quickly reopened the bakery at Oronoco and Water Streets after
the fire, and he promptly pursued more community relations and more diversified interests. He was made Warden of the First Ward from 1798 to 1799,
and a trustee of the poor and work house from 1806 to 1807 (Miller 1992a).
He also became a more active church and community member, and his name
appears often as a signatory to various local initiatives.

Recall that during the 1790s financial institutions evolved rapidly. By late
in the decade, many along the Alexandria waterfront were indebted to the
Bank of Alexandria. To secure payments for these loans, it was not unusual for
people to mortgage properties and other possessions. There was still a considerable amount of credit extended to individuals within the community,
even by banks, due to the general lack of hard currency in circulation. Despite
the passage of the Bank and Coinage Acts, it would take decades for the work-
ings of a cash economy to coalesce. Circumstances forced people to pursue
creative means of financing their endeavors, and equally creative means to
avoid creditors. It was common practice in the late eighteenth century to

transfer lands and property frequently among friends, neighbors, and family, either as collateral against debts, to seize on some opportunity, or just to obtain immediate cash. Real estate holdings might be transferred back and forth between neighbors several times in one month, each using it to back a payment, or to provide cover from creditors. This interdependence among households gave them some independence from the larger forces of commerce (Dawley 1976).

Alternative activities provided yet another means of economic survival. In addition to being a baker, Andrew Jamieson achieved some of his initial financial success through expansion and subdivision of waterfront lots in Alexandria. By order of the Alexandria Board of Trustees, "Every purchaser of riverside lots by the terms of sale was to have the benefit of extending said lots into the river so far as they shall think proper without any obstruction from the street called Water Street" (Ring and Pippenger 1995).[2] When Alexander Henderson had purchased Lot 31 to open a Glassford & Company store, the eastern portions of Lot 31 fronted on Water Street and the Potomac River, where there were twelve- to fourteen-foot cliffs above the shore. In January of 1778, Henderson conveyed the property to William Herbert, a prominent Alexandria merchant. Beginning in 1782, when the city approved legislation, the bluffs of the Potomac River were cut back and the shallow mud flats along the shoreline were filled by sinking derelict ships and timber cribbing full of fill debris (Shomette 1985). Through this process North Union Street was laid out in 1784, and by the turn of the nineteenth century the Alexandria riverfront from Queen to Cameron Streets had been extended several hundred feet eastward into what had once been the Potomac River. By 1799 the shoreline had moved so far eastward that the new lots were being subdivided and sold (figures 5.1 and 5.2). The tailor George K. Wise moved his residence to the new Lot 17. Although it didn't happen for a number of years, a bakery was eventually built on the new Lot 10, which became the archaeological site.

Between the years 1801 and 1815, Alexandria's annual exports averaged about $1,114,000 per year, or eight times that of its neighbor, Georgetown, a few miles upriver (Duffy 1965; Hurst 1991; Macoll and Stansfield 1977). Those first decades of the nineteenth century were a difficult time to be a craftsman. The yellow fever epidemic in 1803, coupled with severe weather droughts and a shortage of local capital threw the once thriving port of Alexandria into serious decline. In 1807, President Thomas Jefferson issued

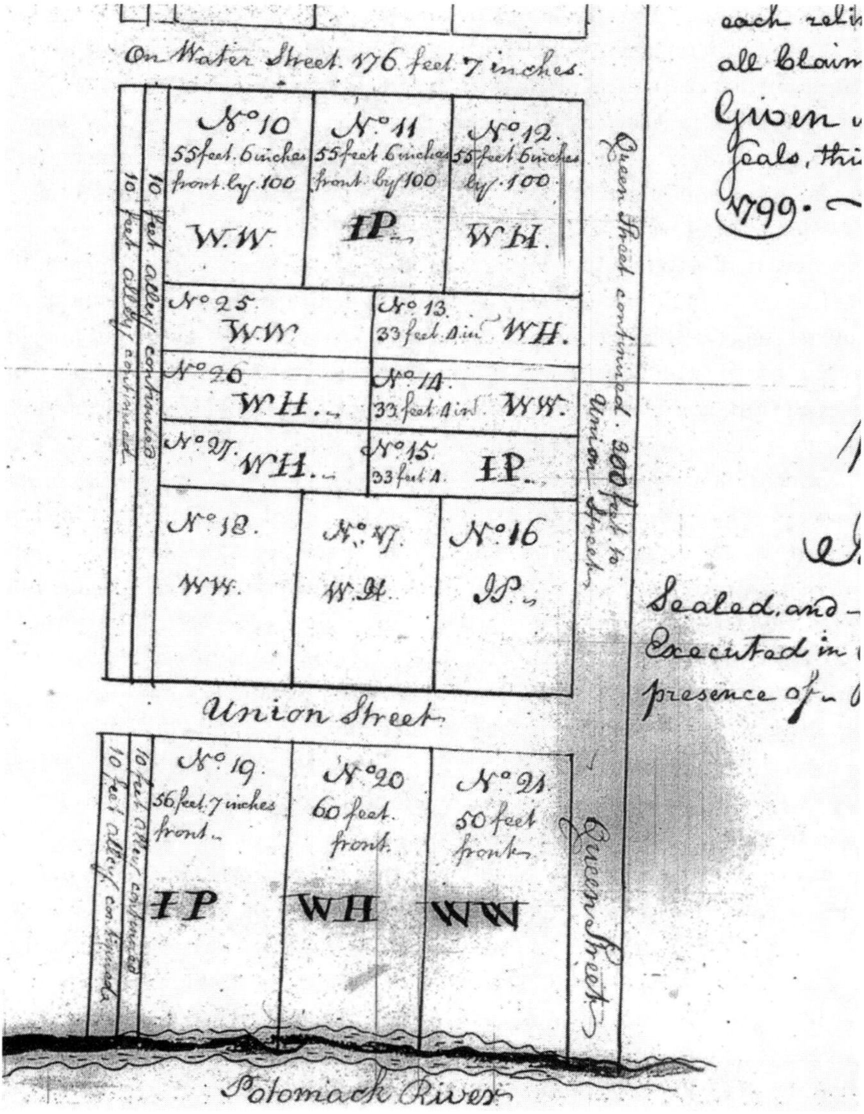

On Water Street. 176 feet 7 inches.

Nº 10	Nº 11	Nº 12
55 feet 6 inches front by 100	55 feet 6 inches front by 100	55 feet 6 inches by 100
W.W	IP	W.H.

10 feet alley continued

Nº 25 W.W	Nº 13 33 feet 1 in. W.H.
Nº 26 W.H.	Nº 14 33 feet 1 in. W.W.
Nº 27 W.H.	Nº 15 33 feet 1. IP.

Nº 18.	Nº 17.	Nº 16
W.W.	W.H.	IP.

Queen Street continued. 300 feet to Union Street.

Union Street.

10 feet alley continued

Nº 19	Nº 20	Nº 21
56 feet 7 inches front	60 feet front.	50 feet front
IP	WH	WW

Queen Street.

Potomack River.

each reli
all claim
Given
feals, thi
1799.

Sealed, and
Executed in
presence of

FIGURE 5.1.
Plat of Lot 31 subdivision from 1799, showing layout of new lots and the new Potomac shoreline. Lot 10 at upper left is where the steam bakery was built.

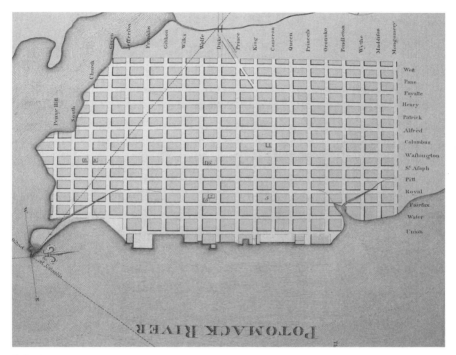

FIGURE 5.2.
Thomas's map of Alexandria from 1798 after the majority of build-out along the river.

his Embargo Act, which closed American ports to the French and British during the Napoleonic War. The town was further hampered when the disastrous
fire of 1810 ravaged its waterfront and destroyed dozens of commercial buildings and businesses. Furthermore, Alexandria was captured and held for ran-
som by the British during the War of 1812 (actually August, 1814) and its
warehouses were pilfered by the enemy, who commandeered $50,000 worth of
flour, tobacco, and cotton (Miller 1998). Alexandria's economy suffered substantially as a result, and its financial institutions incurred serious losses.

That period was especially difficult for bakers, in part because of the overall economy, but also because their business became increasingly regulated. In
1807, the Alexandria Council enacted legislation designed to address the danger of fire that bakeries supposedly posed to the community. The order was
basically a building code, and stated that "Sundry inhabitants of the town rel-
ative to the establishment of a bakehouse at the foot of King Street, be referred

to Messrs. Smith, McKinney & Hewes, who shall take the same into consideration, and also the situation of the various bakehouses in town, the materials of which they are built, and the probable danger which the neighborhood incurs from fire."[3]

The economic hardships led to some creative tactics for evading creditors. In 1814 the real estate dealer William Wilson transferred ownership of all his household furniture to his neighbor William Herbert, a prominent merchant, to secure payment of his debts to Andrew Jamieson (Wardell 1989). Besides clever ways to avoid creditors or obtain capital cash, people were devising creative methods for expanding and reorganizing their businesses. Jamieson made some of his income from the expansion of waterfront lots. The process reclaimed land and resulted in wharves extending to the deep water channel, making waterfront businesses more accessible to ships and facilitating the convergence between manufacturers and shippers. Joshua West advertised in 1817 the sale of good coal on board the *Antelope* at Jamieson's wharf.[4]

URBAN ALEXANDRIA LABOR

Throughout that time, Andrew Jamieson remained a large slave owner by Alexandria standards. Baking had once been a craft, with a master and an apprentice or two, and maybe a few others. The expansion of baking operations during the war and afterward involved the addition of slave labor and less role for the craftsman. The city of Alexandria has always maintained a duality of positions with regard to slavery. With its proximity to the U.S. Congress, the city was always a center of debate regarding emancipation and slavery. Alexandria was home to active abolitionists and had a large Quaker population that was appalled by the practice. At the same time, the city also had slave trading businesses like Franklin and Armfield or Price Birch & Company (Artemel et al. 1987).[5] Slaves in the Alexandria urban setting were generally domestics for merchants, but some carried out labor, such as those for Jamieson. In the 1810 census of Alexandria there were 1,488 slaves and 836 free blacks (Artemel et al. 1987). In that census, forty-six slaves were specifically identified as "bakers," seventeen female and twenty-nine male (Deines 1994). Bakers were thus 3.9 percent of the enslaved population in 1810. Censuses between 1800 and 1850 show slaves making up 23 to 29 percent of Alexandria's population, with free blacks making up about 2.4 percent.[6] The average number of slaves owned by bakers was roughly two each (Pritchett 1993). Andrew Jamieson owned eighteen, making him the second largest slaveholder in the city next to ship carpenter John Hunter (Deines 1994).

In urban settings like Alexandria, slaves often lived in separate homes. As one example, Joseph Thomas was listed in the 1810 census as a baker and slave, and also as a head of a household containing twelve slaves. Although enslaved himself, Thomas was assessed taxes in 1810–1812 for one tythable, essentially a head of household tax, as well as tax on the one story structure they lived in (Veloz 1978). At that time there were ten bakeries in Alexandria, but Thomas may have worked for Jamieson since he was among the largest slaveholders. In addition, apprenticeship indentures for Alexandria include at least seventy-nine individuals who were apprenticed to bakers (table 5.2; Miller 1991, 1992b).

Urban areas tended to foster freedoms for blacks that the countryside plantations didn't (e.g., Leone 2005). The plantation model of permanent lifelong

Table 5.2. Alexandria bakery apprentices. Based on Miller (1998).

John Audley	Thomas Spencer	William Butler
Jacob Beld	George Tyler	William Carpenter
Garret Bowling	Samuel Vanhorn	James Carter
James Carter	McKenzie Waugh	Robert Carter
Robert Carter	John Wiley	Patrick Connall
James Crawford	Michael Wilkes	William Conner
Christopher Duffey	Anthony Williams	John Coode
Isaac Fouch	Shedrick Adams	Edward Evans
John Frazer	Ignatius Butler	Victor Fleury
Edward Gird	William Butler	Daniel Fox
George Goods	Charles Henry Coxall	John Gavin
John Hampson	Lemuel Crandell	Alfred Gibson
William Hunter	William Devaughn	James Grandison Grimes
Archibald Jackson	John Hodgkin	Joseph Grimes
David Jones	William Johnson	Peyton Hines
Caleb Lomax	Samuel McGee	William Hooper
John McClae	John Mara	Henry Kincaid
John Mara	James Montgomery	James Mulrooney
Richard Miller	David Rowlinson	Charles Henry Peake
William Mills	William Roysan	Martin Power
Thomas Morgan	John Seidle	James Purley
Charles Philips	John Sinclair	William Simpson
James Rix	William Wallace	Daniel Stor
Daniel Slimmer	Alloysius Baggett	Joseph Thomas
John Storman	Robert Bell	Elias Thompson
John Swylor	John Bowles	
James Taylor	John A. Bryan	

servitude for slaves was not the case in urban Chesapeake areas like Alexandria. Northern Virginia and Washington, D.C., were relatively tolerant of free blacks compared to southern Virginia, and Alexandria saw a steady growth in that population. In 1820 the city's slave population was 1,408, while the free population was 1,168. By 1830 those numbers had changed to 1,381 enslaved and 1,201 free.[7] The same phenomenon was taking place in Annapolis. The population of Annapolis remained roughly a third black into the nineteenth century. However, by 1820 the black population of 917 was 43 percent free (Leone 2005). The factors that fostered urban freedoms are not entirely clear. It is certain that it was linked to the new social and business patterns of urban areas like Alexandria and Annapolis, including different methods for procuring and organizing labor within manufacturing.

The buying and selling of labor was common in early nineteenth-century urban settings and often followed the system of term contracts used for white indentures (Galenson 1981; McCormac 1904; Preisser 1982). We know the names of many slaves owned by Andrew Jamieson because he freed them. Jamieson favored the use of *slave indentures*, in which an enslaved individual worked for a number of years and then was sold or freed. These transactions recorded valuable information about the individuals and the dynamics of slavery in the urban Alexandria setting. For example, in 1800, Andrew Jamieson manumitted Robert Davis (Dennee 2001). In 1805 Jamieson emancipated Winny when Charles Nix, a free man of color, paid for her emancipation (Wardell 1989). In 1807 Jamieson freed David, in accordance with the provisions of David's purchase ten years earlier. In 1802 Jamieson had purchased Abraham for five years' service from Daniel McLean, and Abraham was freed with certification of his good behavior on December 16, 1807 (Wardell 1989). In November 1811, Rachel was bought from Andrew Jamieson by Mordecai Miller and freed right away. Other names found in the city records include Sylvia, John Brown, William Norton, and Mary Ann Stoutly and her children Sampson and Clara. Each must have had a compelling story that is also connected to Jamieson and the Alexandria baking industry. Baking labor in Alexandria was obviously not organized in a free market system, and yet the slave indenture system was also not the most punishing kind of permanent servitude described for other settings, like plantations.

We get a sense for Jamieson's business competition in Alexandria, as well as some of the day-to-day operations of bakeries, from the pages of the *Alexandria*

Gazette. John Young, a local baker, had an unfortunate experience when lightning struck his bake house on Union Street in July 1811 and killed Bowie, an employee.[8] In 1817, baker James MacDonald "informed his friends & the public in general that he had commenced loaf bread baking at Royal Street."[9] F. McClellan, who commenced the baking business in 1820, commented that "she had hired an expert man as a baker from Philadelphia. She intends to devote part of her time to baking mutton, pies, tarts of every description."[10] Apparently Alexandria bakers specialized in many different products, but people throughout Maryland and Virginia often described what a treat it was to have "a keg of Jamieson's crackers."[11]

Andrew Jamieson knew the difficulties of labor management and had seen the impending mechanization of the baking profession coming. He was a new breed of baker, different from previous generations, and already accustomed to being a manager more than a craftsman. In a rudimentary way he was buying labor, in the sense that he was contracting multiyear terms from African Americans and (presumably white) indentures. It was done under the rubric of slavery, but with an agreement that included set term limits and provided incentives to both Jamieson and the individuals that worked for him. In 1806 Andrew Jamieson had observed a demonstration of an invention that would actually change the long-standing methods of baking. It was a new oven. Jamieson wrote a testimony for the newspaper:

> These are to certify to all whom it may concern, that I, Andrew Jamieson, biscuit baker in the town of Alexandria, and district of Columbia, was in the town of Fredericksburg, in the state of Virginia, some time since the middle of last January, and there did see the operation of biscuit baking in the new invented oven in the possession of Messrs. Richard and Stephen Winchester, of Fredericksburg, which oven I have every reason to believe the sole invention of Mr. James Deneale, of Dumfires, in the state of Virginia, and hereby declare and aver that I saw said New Invented or Perpetual Oven bake large and small biscuits in as short a time and as regular a manner as an oven I have seen these forty years I have been at the baking business. Given under my hand this sixth day of February (in Alexandria, and district of Columbia) in the year one thousand eight hundred six. (*Alexandria Daily Advertiser,* Wednesday, July 22, 1807, p. 3)

This new technology was an oven that stayed warm. By the old manner, dough was put in the oven when the oven was at its hottest, and the dough cooked as the oven cooled. Deneale's invention moved the fire *out* of the oven itself. In terms of preparation, this eliminated the task of splitting the cord wood into small pieces. It also allowed the oven to be continuously heated at a steady temperature while products were inside cooking. Deneale said he would construct one of his ovens twenty feet in length and three feet six inches in width for $500. In the same advertisement, Robert Hartshorne of New York attested that he has been successfully using the patent oven at his bakery in New York City. Andrew Jamieson expanded his firm not long afterward. In 1812 Jamieson opened a second bakery at Ramsay's Wharf at the foot of King Street, where he manufactured bread and biscuits. That biscuit bakery was a three-story operation that likely utilized biscuit preparation machines tended by enslaved or indentured labor.

By 1821, the Jamieson baking business is referred to as Andrew Jamieson & Son. That is when Robert Jamieson had joined the firm (Miller 1995). A manufacturing census from the time shows that Andrew Jamieson & Son employed seven men, no women, and five boys. Major equipment at the bakery included a dough trough, Leser, moulding boards, and dockey (it is unclear what a Leser or dockey are). The articles manufactured at the bakery were listed as crackers. Under the heading "general remarks concerning the establishment" was written "formerly a large business, but now very circumscribed." It is signed Robert Jamieson for Andrew Jamieson. Andrew posted a notice in the newspaper that apprentice Thomas Stevenson had escaped, so the men and boys listed in the survey were a mix of enslaved and indentured labor.[12] The "circumscribed" nature is probably a reflection of the weak economy, new federal and city regulations, and the competition among the many bakers within Alexandria. An inventory of bakers in Alexandria between 1820 and 1830 identified eighteen (table 5.3).

Table 5.3.   Alexandria bakers, 1820–1830.

Elizabeth Baggett	Frederick Koones
Frederick Churchman	Hugh Leddy
John Churchman	James McDonald
Thomas Crandle	Margaret McDonald
John Cranston	Samuel Magee
William Devaughn	John S. Mills
Peter Hewett	Henry W. Nicholson
Andrew Jamieson	Anthony Rhodes
Robert Jamieson	John Tatspaugh

In 1823 Andrew died and Robert became the sole proprietor of the business (Miller 1997). The year after Andrew's death, his wife Mary Jamieson died, and Robert married Catherine Porter Sanford (Pippenger 2001).[13] The couple would eventually have five sons. It was also in the 1820s, when the city's financial situation transformed into Alexandria's "golden age of commerce," and new growth (Hurst 1991:2). Robert apparently knew the value of politics, which his father had learned the hard way. Besides his baking establishments, Robert Jamieson was well integrated into the political and business fabric of the Alexandria community (Miller 1997). He was elected to the Common Council in 1823, served as president of the Exchange Bank, and was a prominent stockholder in the Mount Vernon Cotton Factory. From 1826 almost continuously to 1840 he served as Ward 1 Councilman, an office he shared with one of his father's old business partners Robert Anderson.

THE JAMIESON STEAM BAKERY

Most American industry was expanding in the second quarter of the nineteenth century and Robert Jamieson, with his business acumen and access to financial capital, clearly had ideas for expanding production of Andrew Jamieson & Son baking. The so-called Industrial Revolution in America was a dynamic phenomenon that included investment in specialized tools, machines, and facilities to regularize production. It required an expansion of cash markets for products, and resulted in a streamlining of production processes to reduce dependence on skilled labor. All were reliant on the establishment and valuation of a U.S. currency and an increased integration of regional economic forces.

In 1832 Robert Jamieson paid brickmason and carpenter Hugh Carolin $2,700 for two lots on the east side of North Water Street between Cameron and Queen Streets, and an additional $1,500 to construct a three-story bakery (figure 5.3; Miller 1998).[14] This is the location that ultimately became archaeological site 44AX180. The location was part of the original town Lot 31, coincidentally the same lot that had been purchased by Alexander Henderson for Glassford & Company five decades earlier (see chapter 4).

The new Jamieson's Bakery at 35 North Water Street was ranked as Alexandria's fifth largest business from 1832 to 1865 (Hurst 1991).[15] When the new bakery opened in 1832 it was on the cusp of steam power popularity. The use of steam engines in Alexandria was growing rapidly in the early 1830s due to

FIGURE 5.3.
Photograph of Jamieson's steam bakery, ca. 1864, taken facing northeast from Green's
Mansion House Hotel roof (see Smith and Miller 1989).

a local manufacturer. Thomas Smith advertised that his business was in operation at a foundry on Potomac and Wolfe Streets, and he would "execute or-
ders for mill work & castings of every description, and high and low pressure
steam engines and machinery in general" (Miller n.d.).[16] Completed in 1831,
Thomas W. Smith & Company's first engine was a ten-horsepower high-
pressure model that he used in his own factory.[17] Smith is the likely supplier
of Jamieson's steam engines, and his company continued to make high and
low pressure steam engines throughout the mid-nineteenth century (Miller n.d.).

In terms of the baking industry, Jamieson appears to have pioneered the
use of steam power and large scale mechanization in Alexandria. For Robert
Jamieson, the means were at hand in 1832 to upgrade his business, a move
that set him apart from other bakers. He was well-connected socially and politically, and could easily obtain capital for investment. He had seen his father's
baking business evolve from simple craft workshops to small-scale use of

mechanized processes. Robert Jamieson was an established businessman, the economy had improved, and the Smith steam engines were available virtually next door. Every manufacturer seemed to be buying one. Thomas Swann's plaster mill got a ten-horsepower engine, and there were two six-horsepower engines for the tan bark mills of Joseph Miller and Charles and James Smoot (Sharrer 1977). In addition, Smith manufactured a fifteen-horsepower engine to power the saws and lathes at the James Green cabinet factory at the southeast corner of Prince and Fairfax Streets. The largest engine manufactured at the Smith plant was an engine of twenty horsepower for Drummond's plaster and bark mill in Norfolk in 1833. Another large one was supplied for the Alexandria Canal Company in 1834 (Sharrer 1977). Robert Jamieson added to this mechanization of industry, and was probably one of the only bakers in Alexandria who could afford taking risks on this new technology. The city directory of 1834 lists eleven bakers and Jamieson was not among them (table 5.4; Matthews 1988). The list indicates a continued level of competition existed among bakers in Alexandria. It also underscores the fact that Jamieson had made the transition to industrial capitalist. His bakery was the fifth largest business in the city but Jamieson himself no longer classified as a baker.

Throughout history, bakers have faced public criticisms, and price-fixing and collusion are among the most common. In 1833, as mechanization was growing, hard choices were being weighed between the use of slave labor and the cost of machines and facilities. In that year the Alexandria baking industry again faced a round of charges that local bakers were engaged in collusion by setting prices. Price-fixing charges were leveled against bakers in most cities, and probably had some merit (Middleton 2001). Of course, the charges were quickly denied by the bakers in Alexandria, who then complained openly about the high price of baker's flour.[18] Also in 1833, an anonymous letter to

Table 5.4.   Alexandria bakers listed in the 1834 Alexandria City Directory.

Elizabeth Baggot	Robert Henry
John Churchman	Hugh Leddy
John Creighton	Joel Reynolds
Wm. Egan	John Tatspaugh
Peter Hewitt	Simon Turley
Charles Henry	

the editor in the *Alexandria Gazette* set forth an argument for the need for factories and manufacturing investment.[19] There was a sentiment that Alexandria might lose its advantage if it didn't modernize by investing in manufacturing and discouraging slavery. The accusations and the letters to the editor are signs of Alexandria's changing economic situation. They also highlight the fact that Jamieson's 1832 steam bakery was a forerunner for change.

The corollary to mechanization was the use of labor in production, and specifically that of slaves. The use of machinery had a monetary cost associated with it, but slavery had an ethical cost. The implications of slave labor and states rights were in the fore of public debate in the 1830s, and Alexandria, which was part of the District of Columbia and home to many government officials, was a major battleground of the antislavery movement. An 1836 antislavery broadside published in New York ridiculed Alexandria, showing images of the Franklin & Armfield slave pen on Duke Street (American Anti-Slavery Society 1836). Articles in the *Alexandria Gazette* had argued for years of the superiority of free labor over enslaved labor (Crothers 2005; Hickin 1971; Janney 1844). The practice of Andrew Jamieson in the first quarter of the century of contracting term labor in periods of five or ten years suggests that the Presbyterian businessmen of Alexandria were in fact ahead of their time. Manufacturers were not only ready to explore new labor relations but had already forged ahead, establishing their own system of African American labor tenure. Many arguments for emancipation were tied to the rapidly spreading evangelical religions such as Methodism, which clearly denounced slavery as evil (e.g., *The North Star* 1848). A Virginia minister from Loudoun County named Samuel Janney was active in the abolition movement and wrote editorials to the *Alexandria Gazette* espousing the advantages of emancipation and encouraging manufacturing (see the appendix). Janney's message was placed in the *Alexandria Gazette* knowing it would receive a proper reception. In the urban setting of Alexandria, the issue of slave labor was closely tied to the economics of manufacturing, including the availability of a free labor pool and the prevailing attitudes about using wage labor. The same year that Robert Jamieson opened his new bakery at 35 North Water Street, he freed a substantial number of his slaves, including Kitty White, age thirty-one, Francis Washington, age forty-one, Joseph Feirel, age forty-one, Peter Brown, age twenty-nine, and Albert Rookard, aged twenty-four (Dennee 2001).

As the use of steam power was refined and improved, Jamieson upgraded his machinery accordingly. To expand his business in 1843, Jamieson purchased a fifty-five by one-hundred-foot parcel on the north side of the bakery. The 1850 commercial census for Alexandria indicates that Robert Jamieson utilized a twelve-horsepower steam engine at his bakery. It powered a system of pulleys and belts that operated a Ferris wheel–like apparatus for the manufacture of bread and biscuits. According to the "1850 Census of Manufacturers" the enterprise was valued at $24,950; employed sixteen men and utilized 4,900 barrels of flour and one hundred tons of coal (1850 Census of Manufacturers for the City of Alexandria; Hurst 1991). The Thompson's business directory for 1851–1852 listed Jamieson & Co., on Water Street, as bakers of ship's bread and biscuits. All other bakers are in a separate category as bakers of loaf bread (*Thompson's* 1852). Alexandria City tax records show that the tax assessment for Jamieson's bakery jumped between 1853 and 1854 from $5,500 to $8,000, probably when the steam engine was upgraded. The timing of those upgrades coincided with other critical components to expand the business. By 1853 there was a steam powered flour mill at the foot of Duke Street, and the city's public water system had been established, providing this critical element of the business in a more reliable way.

ARCHAEOLOGY AT JAMIESON'S BAKERY

Excavations at the site of the 1832 steam bakery uncovered numerous features of Jamieson's complex. In Alexandria the site is called the Lee Street site. A total of thirty-seven bakery features were identified during excavations that included four separate bakery buildings and features like brick walls with stone foundations and the bases of four ovens in a row. Evidence was found of an elaborate water management system that included a cistern and three wells, as well as a trench and pipe system below the floor for circulating hot steam (figure 5.4). Like the 99 Main Street site in Annapolis, the Lee Street site represented complex urban archaeology (figure 5.5). The site number assigned by the state—44AX180—includes an area of 49,422 square feet within the city, and the site contained evidence of multiple occupation phases over several hundred years (Cuddy et al. 2006). A total of 67,042 artifacts were collected, cataloged, and conserved for research, originating from wharfs, taverns, houses, and a Civil War camp. Jamieson's Bakery was only one element of this complex site.

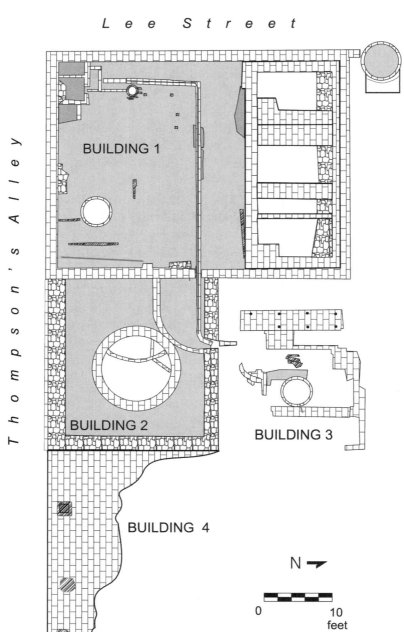

L e e   S t r e e t

T h o m p s o n ' s   A l l e y

BUILDING 1

BUILDING 2

BUILDING 3

BUILDING 4

N ➤

0   10
feet

FIGURE 5.4.
Archaeological features of the Jamieson's Bakery.

According to historical accounts, the main bakery structure, Building 1, included the kneading boards and breaks, molds, and ovens. The archaeological excavations located the foundation of Building 1, which measured forty-five by thirty-five feet. Excavation revealed the construction techniques, which had begun with the placement of a mudsill, topped with dry-laid stones, with bricks placed atop the stone. The stones were 2 feet high and approximately 1.5 feet thick. Five courses of brick remained on top of the stones and traces of plaster were found on their interior. These construction methods are typical of the time and place.

The artifacts recovered in the area of Building 1 are generally indicative of the early nineteenth century. A total of 347 ceramic fragments with diagnostic styles were recovered from the bakery area and include both refined and utilitarian wares (table 5.5). Glazed coarse earthenwares comprise the largest type at 36 percent. Pearlware is the next largest group, followed by creamware and whiteware. The higher percentage of utilitarian wares, such as the coarse earthenwares, would be expected from the commercial nature of the property. It is important to note, however, that the bakery sits on landfill from when Lot 31 was expanded westward into the Potomac River in the late eighteenth

Table 5.5. Summary of ceramics from Jamieson's Bakery. Dates are from Miller (2000); end dates in the twentieth century have been capped at 1900 based on the site context.

Coarse earthenware, glazed	124	35.7	1630–1800
Pearlware	59	17	1779–1830
Creamware	39	11.2	1762–1820
Whiteware	32	9.2	1805–1900
Unidentified	20	5.8	—
Coarse earthenware, unglazed	16	4.6	—
Gray salt-glazed stoneware	9	2.6	1705–1900
Ironstone	9	2.6	1813–1900
Buff smooth-glazed stoneware	9	2.6	1700–1810
White paste refined earthenware	5	1.4	1842–1900
Brown smooth-glazed stoneware	4	1.1	1733–1750
Hard paste porcelain	4	1.2	1768–1900
Bone china	4	1.1	1794–1900
Brown salt-glazed stoneware	3	0.9	1671–1775
Smooth-glazed stoneware	2	0.6	1720–1805
Buff and gold stoneware	2	0.6	—
Possible creamware	2	0.6	1762–1820
Tin-glazed earthenware	1	0.3	1628–1800
Yellowware	1	0.3	1830–1900
Rockingham	1	0.3	1830–1900
Refined redware	1	0.3	—

century. The ceramics recovered at the site come from a broad range of time periods, and it was difficult to tell which pieces may have existed on the lot prior to the bakery, what originated from the bakery construction, and which may have been deposited later. Overall the artifact counts from the bakery are relatively low (table 5.6). Many objects were recovered from other areas of the large Lee Street site, or from fill deposits that were not associated with the bakery. A large proportion of botanical remains were recovered from the exterior well. If these are discounted from the overall totals, then architectural materials were the most common type of artifact, followed by kitchen items, and then faunal remains.

The base of the ovens for Jamieson's bakery was uncovered by excavations in the north end of Building 1. The ovens clearly indicate a shift in the baking industry toward large-scale bulk manufacturing. The entire oven area measured fifteen by thirty-five feet. The ovens were constructed of bricks laid with mortar and divided into four separate oven pits. Ovens 1, 2, and 4, numbered from west to east, measured five by eleven feet; oven 3 measured two by eleven feet. A description from 1870 indicates that these ovens would have reached all the way to the third floor, providing an area where crackers could be dried.[20] The four ovens would have presumably opened onto each of the three floors of the main bakery chamber so that crackers could be loaded into the ovens. The northern end of the oven foundations was a French drain, an architectural element probably designed to aid in cleaning the ovens.

Of particular interest, excavations of the bakery complex revealed an extensive water supply system. The water system was necessary largely to feed

Table 5.6.   Historic artifacts from the site of Jamieson's Bakery in Alexandria.

Artifacts Category	Count	%
Floral	17,300	68.59
Architectural	5,758	22.83
Kitchen	810	3.21
Faunal	459	1.82
Miscellaneous	313	1.24
Activities	270	1.07
Clothing	237	0.94
Furniture	43	0.17
Personal	17	0.07
Tobacco	16	0.06
Total	25,223	100

the steam-powered mechanisms that replaced the manual labor of baking. During the eighteenth and nineteenth centuries in urban areas like Alexandria and Annapolis, sources of clean water became increasingly essential to both residences and businesses as population densities increased. In Alexandria, water could be obtained from private and public cisterns, wells and reservoirs, and from the Potomac River. Fresh water was especially important to establishments involved in food production. Jamieson's bakery would have consumed large volumes of water in food preparation, water as fuel for the steam engine, and water for the cleaning of cooking equipment.

The water system included three wells and a filtration cistern placed throughout the bakery. The cistern, in particular, reflects a specific moment in time in urban Chesapeake towns. Cisterns were designed to catch and filter water, and they generally date to the first half of the nineteenth century. In 1797, residents of Alexandria were severely hit by yellow fever, and again in 1804 (Hurst 1991). The city well water was blamed as the source of numerous illnesses, and it spurred an interest in trying to purify the water (Perge 1980;

FIGURE 5.5.
Archaeologists and volunteers excavate the ovens at the site of the steam bakery on Lee Street. (Photograph courtesy of the Alexandria Archaeology Museum, Alexandria, Virginia.)

Shephard 1988). Both Alexandria and Annapolis were planning municipal water systems in the 1840s. Cisterns reflect a time between the influx of diseases, such as yellow fever in the 1790s, and the implementation of municipal water supplies, approximately 1850.

The circular cistern at Jamieson's Bakery was set into the floor in Building 2, which was a two-story structure twenty-five by twenty-eight feet attached to the back of the main bakery building (figure 5.6). The cistern had an interior diameter of thirteen feet, and the walls were constructed of mortared brick three courses wide, making the cistern 1.5 feet thick. Multiple coats of plaster covered the brick surfaces on the interior of the cistern, presumably sand-lime cement which was used as a waterproofing compound throughout the nineteenth century (Abell and Glumac 1997). The cistern had four interior chambers, two large and two small, through which the water was filtered. Extending away from the cistern were curving brick alignments that channeled overflow water into one of the wells that was in the engine room.

There was a well inside Building 1 that would have provided a ready water source for the baking process. The remains of a third well were found outside

FIGURE 5.6.
Photograph of the top of the cistern after excavations. (Photograph courtesy of the Alexandria Archaeology Museum, Alexandria, Virginia.)

the bakery at the northwest corner of Building 1, along with a portion of a foundation wall for the well housing. Among other things, this well contained a total of 17,120 botanical remains, which included mostly seeds and seed fragments, six nut fragments, and one wood fragment (Cuddy et al. 2006). With the exception of the wood, all botanical remains likely result from food waste disposal, and the majority date from the Civil War period, not the period of the bakery's occupation.

Another aspect of the water system was the boiler and drain that fed the steam engine. A small rectangular chamber in the southwestern corner of Building 1 was the location of the firebox. Recessed into the dirt floor of the building was the top of a wooden barrel. The firebox housed a boiler for the steam system. The barrel was connected to the firebox by a long wooden trough, recessed into the ground. The trough and barrel functioned as the boiler drainage system.

Understanding the steam system at Jamieson's Bakery was a central goal of the archaeology. Evidence for the location of the steam engine was found in Building 3, which was the engine room. It had a brick and wood floor, and on the west side was a platform of brick fifteen by four feet that was the engine platform. Four pairs of metal pins ran the length of the brick platform and functioned as mounting bolts for the steam engine. The engine itself would have been a long, somewhat linear shape that would fit this mounting. Jamieson probably had a locally made engine; however, the Thompson's Automatic Governor Cut-off Engine of 1849 produced by the Buckeye Engine Company (1849) of Ohio fits the same general description of the engine mount and is presented here as an illustration (figure 5.7). The Thompson's engine could produce forty pounds of pressure per square inch and consumed an estimated 18.76 pounds of water per horsepower, per hour.

The steam engine provided power that was diverted to belt-driven devices inside the bakery. The machines would take dough and stamp out racks of crackers quickly and uniformly. A person tended the machine, probably adding the dough and controlling the pace of the production. Although a person was needed with the machine, many more crackers could be formed in the same period of time than the person could by hand. A promotional flyer for the bakery provides a representative image of the process (although this was published in 1873; figure 5.8). Presumably through use of belts and pulleys the engine could power several of these machines simultaneously. After being

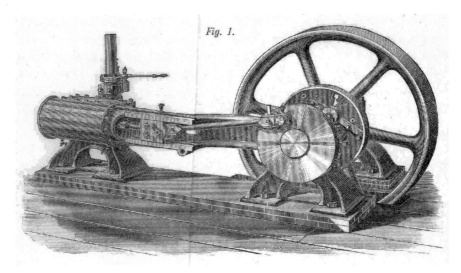

FIGURE 5.7.
Thompson's Automatic Cut-Off Engine (Buckeye Engine Company 1849).

FIGURE 5.8.
Christmas price list from Jamieson's Bakery, 1873. (Courtesy of the Alexandria Library Special Collections.)

formed, many racks of crackers could be stacked into the three-story ovens for baking. The fresh batch of baked crackers could be wrapped and packaged on the upper floors while the dough was prepared for another production run.

The steam engine of the 1800s was a machine that ran on steam, much like the modern internal combustion engine runs on gasoline. High pressure steam for the engine came from the boiler. At Jamieson's bakery a brick-lined channel with a metal pipe running through it ran across Building 1, east to west. Embedded in the floor, this system of pipes conveyed the steam from Building 1 through the bakery to the engine in Building 3. This would have allowed the fire and boiler to be tended from within the main Building 1. The steam would have been piped to the engine, which was housed out back in Building 3. In that location the engine could vent exhausted steam harmlessly into the air without disturbing the working environment of the bakers.

The number of wells at the bakery—three, plus a large cistern—was a safeguard against a water shortage, and allowed the bakery to operate at maximum capacity with few interruptions in production. The Alexandria Water Company began providing citywide water in 1852. Jamieson upgraded his steam engine accordingly, resulting in the increased tax assessment from 1853 to 1854, but probably more production capacity as well.

JAMIESON AND STEAM IN THE MID-NINETEENTH CENTURY

Jamieson's steam bakery of 1832 represents a major step toward a capitalist economy in the United States. There is a great deal of historical documentation available on Robert Jamieson and his father Andrew. Without the information on Andrew from the late eighteenth century, we wouldn't understand the build-up in production toward the steam factory. Without the archaeological research we wouldn't know the functional layout of the bakery. We can now contextualize Jamieson's steam bakery economically and socially, with a realistic perspective on how it operated.

The 1830s was a time of increased use of cash transactions in America (Henretta 1998). In contrast to credit, the implementation of a cash-based economy in the United States would make transactions much easier. The cash economy made timely payment for goods more predictable, and eliminated many risks of long distance trade that allowed manufacturers to venture into new markets in more distant locations. Jamieson's steam bakery emerged at the right time to take advantage of mass production and cash markets. The increased scale of his operation used a mix of strategies to economize on the amount of labor input needed while producing large amounts of products.

By the late 1850s, the Jamieson Bakery was famous as the supplier of crackers for Queen Victoria's court. "Queen Victoria as a young woman so relished them that she imported them for the Royal table" (Miller 1998:28). The city of Alexandria clearly wanted to take credit for Jamieson's accomplishments, as well as that of his father.

> The character of the ship and pilot bread of Alexandria was unrivalled. There were some dozen manufactories of the kind here. . . . The British Government during the wars of the French Revolution obtained large supplies of bread from Alexandria for their fleets in the West Indies. One baker, a good old man, whom some of us yet remember, had so great a reputation that it was said that Crackers with the name of Andrew Jamieson were to be seen at the table of the King of Great Britain. (*Alexandria Gazette*, January 1, 1859)

The increased use of steam engines in the city for manufacturing purposes of all kinds was also noted in the newspapers.

> There are now in daily operation Steam Engines, at the Cotton Factory; the Railroad depot, Smith & Perkins' Rail Road Works; Hunter's Ship Yard; Thompson & Goodhand's Ship Yard; Smith & Wattles's Saw Mill; the Pioneer Mills; the Alexandria Brewery; Thomas's Plaster Mill; Entwisle & Moore's Foundry; Jamieson's Foundry; Jamieson's Bakery; Jenkins's Planing and Sawing Machine; James Green's Saw Mill; C. C. Bradley's Cabinet Factory; Brengle & Baulauff's Wheelwright shop; Nalls & Brother's Carpenter's shop; C. C. Smoot & Son's Tan Yard; in all twenty, that we call to mind. There may be others.[21]

Jamieson's steam bakery was not only large in scale, but reflects a growth in the baking industry from manual labor to mechanization. Robert Jamieson died on April 10, 1862, at age 67. In his will the "3-story brick and slate Bake House and lot on Water Street" was valued at $7,500.[22] He also had a second bakehouse and lot, a three-story brick and slate building on the west side of Union Street between Princess and Oronoco Streets. What happened with Jamieson's bakeries during the Civil War is a mystery. The Union Army commandeered the entire Lee Street block to use as part of a supply depot, and the bakery may have been used to supply troops (Cuddy et al. 2006). A photograph of the bakery, probably taken by Union troops, is one reward from the time of the Civil War and shows the outside of the building as it stood. After the war, Robert Jamieson's son Andrew sold the bakery to George Hill, who operated it for another decade before moving the business to a new location. The steam factory was vacant by 1885 and torn down in 1888 to build new warehouses (Means 1999).

NOTES

1. *Alexandria Gazette*, June 7, 1787.

2. In 1782, the city approved legislation to allow citizens the right to use the waterfront of their property for whatever purpose they wanted. Most built wharves into the river to capture the shipping trade (Shomette 1985).

3. Quote is from the *Alexandria Gazette*, February 2, 1807. Note that the newspaper by this time had changed its name, dropping the *Columbia Mirror* portion and staying simply with *Alexandria Gazette*. Periodic editorials in the newspapers chronicle the ongoing dialogue about fires and public safety, with frequent reference to the baking industry.

4. In the *Alexandria Gazette*, January 18, 1817.

5. Franklin and Armfield established their slave trading business on Duke Street in 1824 to take advantage of the regional downsizing in slaveholdings. They purchased slaves from northern Virginia plantations that wished to be rid of them and shipped them south, mostly to New Orleans, where demand remained high. Price Birch & Company moved to Alexandria from Washington, D.C., in 1858.

6. The information cited here is from Washington, D.C., censuses. Alexandria remained under the aegis of the federal government as part of Washington, D.C., from 1801 until it was retroceded back to Virginia in 1847. In 1852, it acquired city status and secured a new charter.

7. Figures are from Artemel et al. (1987). Note that the figure for free blacks also includes Indians, but their numbers are not specified.

8. *Alexandria Gazette*, July 11, 1811.

9. *Alexandria Gazette*, April 4, 1817.

10. *Alexandria Gazette*, April 22, 1820.

11. *Alexandria Gazette*, June 28, 1877; also see Miller 1987.

12. *Alexandria Gazette*, May 23, 1823.

13. Obituary, *Alexandria Gazette*, July 13, 1824.

14. See Alexandria Deed Book U2, page 163.

15. Water Street was renamed Lee Street in 1873. As a result of the infill and construction of wharves on the shoreline, by 1873 Water Street was three blocks from the river.

16. *Alexandria Gazette*, February 21, 1831.

17. An excellent description of the Smith Foundry appeared in the *Georgetown Metropolitan* in May 1836, as well as Miller (n.d.).

18. *Alexandria Gazette*, January 12, 1833, January 15, 1833.

19. *Alexandria Gazette*, June 19, 1833.

20. *Alexandria Gazette*, January 14, 1870.

21. *Alexandria Gazette*, June 23, 1854.

22. See Alexandria Will Book 8, page 256–57.

6

Capitalism in the Chesapeake

It has been said that capitalism, to be capitalism, must be capitalism-in-production (Wolf 1982:79). With our twenty-first-century information society of white-collar jobs and investment markets, that may no longer be entirely true. But it was true of the late eighteenth century, and into the nineteenth. Basic production activities, often small domestic industries, were intensified in terms of their activities and eventually capitalized in terms of equipment and assets. In 1745, the baker John Chalmers rented a small waterfront workshop in Annapolis and, with very basic tools and little assistance, he supplied local trading vessels with hard baked ship's bread to sustain them on their trans-Atlantic voyages. By 1845, only a hundred years later, the businessman Robert Jamieson was heavily invested in a three-story steam powered bakery in Alexandria that shipped packaged crackers to overseas markets. Many changes took place in the intervening years, changes within the towns, changes in the components of the baking business, and changes in the structure of economy. Merchant trading under way in Europe since the 1500s united distant areas and accelerated the exchange of goods and money. The mechanization of Britain was slowly spreading to America and areas such as the Chesapeake region saw the predominance of agricultural production giving way to the ascent of manufacturing and industry. It was the Industrial Revolution as well as the origins of capitalism.

Economic activity expanded precipitously throughout the trans-Atlantic region. European financial institutions and individual merchants were investing steadily in commodity exchanges and developing new financial instruments to facilitate their trades. The Scottish trading firm Glassford & Company brought a business model to the Chesapeake that worked with the planter mode of production. The Glassford stores were points of convergence between town and plantation, crops and trade goods, domestic and international economy. While the goldsmith Chalmers thought of minting money, Glassford discovered how to facilitate business transactions without it. And yet, this economic activity was heavily rooted in Great Britain, with the financiers coming from places like London, Glasgow, Whitehaven, and Bristol. The American colonies wanted ruling autonomy, and politics and economics were closely intertwined. The American Revolution is often upheld in history as political freedom, but was instigated in many ways by economic actions both European and American.

Change in Chesapeake urban centers came in many forms, and there were a number of threshold events that led to transformation. With so many social, political, and economic changes, the use of sweeping historical explanations like "the Industrial Revolution" or "the rise of capitalism" lead to more questions. We can walk down King Street in Alexandria or Main Street in Annapolis and see the outcomes of history around us. Yet we are left wondering how events unfolded in these towns. Despite their historic appearance, both towns have transformed considerably. Today there is little baking in either Annapolis or Alexandria, but they are two of the oldest Chesapeake towns and they were early centers of industry. We can look around the waterfronts of Annapolis and Alexandria and ask why production developed in those locations when it did. We know historically that the transformation of business included the ownership of property and tools, the ability to leverage labor, and the availability of investment funding. What was it about the urban settings of Annapolis and Alexandria that affected the outcome of those processes? We wonder which stages of manufacturing and production actually happened before the others, and in what ways did they feed into each other? We also wonder how individuals in the towns played a role. How did the wealthy merchants navigate the political upheavals of the Revolution? How did the artisan craftsmen navigate the economic turmoil of post-Revolutionary United States? Amid all these changes, we might ask: at what point was a capitalist economic system in place?

The research presented here has engaged the study of a particular industry—baking—and the stages of its evolution in order to understand in more detail how capitalism and industry arose in Chesapeake urban towns.

The information presented here provides an anthropological view on the interactions of people, politics, and economy over time. In essence, the political economy of the western Chesapeake region is a story of individuals and how they intersected with the major global influences of their time. Adam Smith first brought together the concept of political economy in 1749, pointing out that economic wealth had politicized agendas. Other scholars like Marx later expanded the concept, making an argument that the capitalist economy was all-encompassing, and that the political agendas driving economy affected the social lives of average workers and wage earners. The political economy of the western Chesapeake region involved the transformation of urban artisan craftsmen and merchant traders into business managers, investors, and entrepreneurs. The process had very distinct impacts on the organization of personal time, families, and community living. Individual craftsmen and merchants had to negotiate their roles within society, and that of their businesses, in order to succeed. Their personal choices were linked to the community structure, the business environment, and the opportunities that international economy brought to the towns.

Despite this basic agency and freedom among artisan craftsmen, it is clear that many of the opportunities available for urban producers in Annapolis and Alexandria came at them from overseas. Artisan craftsmen and merchants may have felt empowered at the local scale, but their actions were in many ways *reactions* to an increasingly globalized economy with complex political relations. Major factors affecting the Chesapeake were tied to Europe, such as the monetary benchmarks and the political directives, while the minor ones were local, like the quality of milled wheat flour or the lack of silver coins. For most events in the growing urban centers, economic relationships formed a tangible impact on social structures and activities, influencing neighborhood organization and creating flashpoints of class tension. This research has devoted considerable time to establishing the intellectual ideals and practical conduct of economic transactions in order to underscore this component of the historic background.

Within the larger discussion of political and economic evolution, we also get evidence of baking as an industry. This book is one example of industrial evolution (e.g., Commons 1909). The process of baking is an old and basic human tradition, and it is through the bakeries and bakers discussed here that the broad vectors of historical change can be focused on two towns in the Chesapeake area and the individuals that moved through them. Baking was perhaps not as important historically as some manufacturing industries like iron, ship building, or textiles. However, it was valuable enough to be carried forward through the years, with its production process intensified through successive stages of complexity. Baking probably didn't require as much master skill as other activities like glass blowing or shoemaking. Nevertheless, those who considered themselves bakers were skilled craftsmen in their own right. Many were immigrants from Europe looking for a pursuit that would allow them to live comfortably. For some, like Richard Fleming, the trade didn't work out. For others it was a catalyst to bigger things. To be sure, bakeries did not determine the course of American economic development. At the same time, the baking industry was not disconnected from economic transformations that were taking place throughout the Chesapeake region.

The time period in focus for this research begins before capitalism had become an instituted process, and extends up to that point. This work provides a unique view of the growth and changes that accompanied capitalist developments both within the urban towns and globally. Historians have recognized the need to build a bridge between what we know about colonial artisan craftsmen and what we know of their much-studied industrial successors of the nineteenth century (Daniels 1993; Kulikoff 1993; Merrill 1995). This study predates the era of industrial histories, but the archaeological interpretations and historical contexts provide the structure and detail with which to discuss industrial progression. The chapters of this book are case studies of how bakers—and urban craftsmen in general—adapted to economic growth and change in the eighteenth and nineteenth centuries. The archaeological materials are tangible evidence from actual times and places that document how the baking profession grew as an industry in relation to historical economic growth.

THE GROWING PRODUCTION SECTOR

Production is the overall dynamic here. People subsist through productive activity, and refine those activities into patterned modes of production (e.g., Marx [1867] 1990). Each factor of production—land, capital, labor, and organization—were different depending on the time period involved. The American colonies in the early eighteenth century contributed to an economy whose central focus in terms of products, currency, markets, and social concerns, was Europe. As a result, the colonial economy has been called a consignment (Henretta 1998), in the sense that products were imported for sale but they came from Europe and the money was cycled back to British merchants. We see from this research, however, that there is a small part of that story missing. It was not just sales, but the productive activities that formed the intersection of local individuals and global structure.

The oldest bakery example was the 1745 shop of John Chalmers. While some colonists were traders conducting import and export of commodities, and many others were invested in agrarian production as farmer or planters, Chalmers was a producer. Within the emerging Annapolis urban setting, Chalmers operated a small waterfront workshop that he rented. The facilities were basic, and resembled many other domestic compounds that had one or two buildings on a small lot, along with ancillary structures. The tools of his baking business were basic as well, redware vessels, wood troughs for mixing dough, and an adequate oven. Chalmers was himself the baker, and he was assisted by indentured servants that he supervised, and possibly a few apprentices or slaves as well. His best customers came from the shipping industry, who stocked their vessels with ship's bread, a stable and vital food for overseas traders. Chalmers didn't own much, but he was a producer. He used locally grown resources, processed them in an urban workshop with laborers, and distributed them to a mostly local market while participating to some extent in community affairs. A corporate nature of cooperation dominated. Production techniques were small-scale, relatively simple, and carried out by artisan craftsmen with the skills and desire to do so.

John Chalmers the baker was distinct for his time. Annapolis would attract many more artisan craftsmen in the decades after 1745, producing a wide range of products for a growing capital city. By the 1760s, with the calls for revolution and independence, more craftsmen were needed. The war effort required supplies, and the local population desired items they could no longer obtain through trade. The central challenge to the artisan craftsmen at that time was how to expand the scale of their businesses. The legal parameters had changed. Craftsmen had shrugged off the colonial dictates designed to prevent production and facilitate trade with England. Growth was accomplished through increased scale and organization. The workshops had to become larger, and with larger workshops the craftsman spent more time supervising. The process required a careful negotiation of what was attainable as an urban craftsman and how best to make it work within the town setting.

This era of urban manufacturers is important to study because those craftsmen encapsulate the American social ideals of free agency and inventive entrepreneurship. It was the era of the subsistence-plus economy, when a co-operative attitude of inclusion prevailed. Its economic correlate was the ex-tension of broad credit across the community. When individual bakers worked for themselves, like Chalmers, they retained an element of self-interest in their craft, and those principles were linked into their own produc-tion skills. The subsistence-plus economy of the early eighteenth century did not have the conditions necessary for a wealthy few to exercise a role in eco-nomic management. Production was small-scale and dispersed, and didn't re-quire large amounts of labor or capital input. However, this was changing. The advent of the Georgian worldview, or *age of reason* described so well by Deetz (1977, 1988), and Leone (1988, 2005), was linked with a new American intel-lectual outlook. Capitalism is about ownership, which translates into re-stricted access and personal advantage, best described as exclusionary economics.

CHANGING URBAN ECONOMICS

With the American Revolution the Chesapeake region emerged from an eco-nomic dependency on Britain. The political separation, finalized in 1782, came with the realization that American economy had already changed. Eu-ropean controls were brushed aside starting in the 1760s, and urban produc-ers had turned their attention to manufacturing goods and supplies for the market revolution (Merrill 1995; Peskin 2003). With the war over, artisan craftsmen found themselves at the center of a newly emerging economy. It was the first *New Economy* of the United States, but there was a natural conflict of interest between those who imported foreign goods—the merchants—and those who manufactured similar items at home—the craftsmen (Peskin 2003). Within Annapolis and Alexandria, the reality was a class conflict. Indi-vidual artisan craftsmen found themselves up against government institu-tions, tariffs, and economic momentum that favored large-scale capital investment in mechanized production. Artisan craftsmen had achieved increased output, but they had reached a threshold of organizational transformation. By the 1790s, Federalist political ideals were clearly aligned with the merchant capital and neomercantilist perspectives. Some have said the Constitution favored large-scale production (Dawley 1976). I point to Hamilton's policies of the 1790s as the intellectual foundations that encouraged capital investments in production.

Frederick Grammar's kitchen-bakery, built at 99 Main Street in 1791, was a transitional post-Revolutionary bakery. Built while the U.S. economy was on hold (e.g., McCusker and Menard 1985), this iteration of baking matched the workshop tasks of earlier days with a diversity of functions and services. The Chalmers bakery that it replaced, the workshop compound used by Richard Fleming, was an outmoded relic from a bygone era. When it burned, Grammar replaced it with a new multipurpose facility that could accommodate merchant import-export activities as well as baking. He kept his bakery shop off the back of the large building, and as the owner he rented the other space to his fellow German and merchant Lewis Neth. Much of the building may have functioned as a warehouse. Through this relationship, Grammar had an inside track for supplying merchant vessels with bread, and when he sold his products locally he could offer brandy and other imported goods to go with his baked products. In Alexandria, Andrew Jamieson had a similar interdependence between merchants and other craftsmen, which allowed his baking business to prosper. With those changes came reorganization of operations, growth in scale of supply networks and raw materials, and requisite reorganization of productive labor.

The examples from this research highlight the realignment at the turn of the nineteenth century between the artisan craftsmen and merchants for control over economic production. In response to the war, artisan craftsmen had greatly increased their share and standing within the local economic process, but subsequent policies and events did not favor them and they were quickly displaced by merchant manufacturers. Indeed, the merchants of Annapolis and Alexandria may have encouraged this shift through illegal channels in the late 1790s, seen in numerous suspicious fires during those years. The fires were ostensibly individualized events, but had a cumulative effect that helped generate the new economic system.

America's New Economy had some key architects, such as Hamilton. The aim of Hamilton and others was to establish a self-reliant system of urban industries to augment the extensive agrarian mode of production. However, a national economic transformation was not a process that could be designed and implemented overnight. East Coast American cities had a system in which the worldwide movement of commodities generated a semi-capitalist economy that encouraged investment (e.g., Braudel 1979; Green 1972; Wolf 1982). On the ground, so to speak, the new economy had to evolve and settle into itself as people found their places within it. Weber (1992 [1930]) writes of the Protestant work ethic and the spirit of capitalism, describing how economic change was accompanied by corollary changes in social perceptions of work and family. The ideological implications of economic change are not explored here, except to say that at the turn of the nineteenth century, growth in manufacturing was considered a national interest. There was no labor market and investment capital had not yet engulfed the means of production, but it was starting. Later would be labor power and capital.

SOCIAL ROLES AND IDENTITIES

A consequence of the economic shifts of the 1790s was change in the social roles of the artisan craftsman and baker (e.g., Rock et al. 1995). The model of the small-scale artisan craftsman of the eighteenth century is exemplified here by the baker John Chalmers of the 1740s. He was a skilled craftsman renting a facility in a growing urban area. He did his own skilled work and was able to live adequately in Annapolis for many years. Richard Fleming appears to have maintained a similar existence during the time of the Revolution and through the 1780s, however, by 1789 he was struggling to survive as an independent craftsman. The nature and character of artisan craftsmen was being recast. Fleming represented a former urban social role that no longer worked in the postwar Annapolis environment. The goldsmith Chalmers in Annapolis was literally recasting British and Spanish coins into American ones. The symbolism of that process—forging new qualities in relation to the new political economy—was playing out across society.

At the turn of the nineteenth century, two figures had invented for themselves a new composite social role. Frederick Grammar in Annapolis and Andrew Jamieson in Alexandria were first-generation immigrants who came to the Chesapeake region before the war and started as artisan craftsmen in baking. Both also found ways to elevate their status in the community through diversification of their livelihoods. These two men had business partnerships, so they were not simply artisan craftsmen. Both used their access to investment capital, gained through social alliances and political contacts, to ensure their baking businesses were financed and protected. Grammar built a large facility on the Annapolis waterfront—99 Main Street—and leased part of it to his merchant friend Lewis Neth. Jamieson opened multiple bakeries in Alexandria that made different types of products. He built a wharf on one of his lots to accommodate shipping. He was also part of an intricate network of waterfront merchants and craftsmen who were neighbors, but who relied on each other as business partners, lenders, and collaborators. Both Grammar and Jamieson moved away from the actual work of baking themselves, and presumably into more elaborate forms of management. Grammar still baked, at least part time, while also trading and selling other commodities. Jamieson probably baked as well, but clearly assumed a larger managerial role, building a second bakery and also selling bakery facilities and waterfront lots that he had improved or reclaimed.

The efforts by Grammar and Jamieson are clear examples of class differentiation in postcolonial America. From an urban social system dominated by merchant traders and artisan craftsmen emerged a class of *middle managers.* Frederick Grammar and Andrew Jamieson provide a distinct perspective on the position and motivations of the middle class, and a gauge of how the middle class viewed the social and economic contexts in which they lived. These men had knowledge and experience in the baking trade, but saw that reorganizing their businesses would bring them more of the urban market share. Historical archaeology has seen extensive research from the perspective of the upper social classes and the distribution of social power through knowledge, ideology, and wealth (Leone 1995, 2005). The focus here on production has found an example of social classes expanding from the middle of the social spectrum. This social change was a function of self-enlightened, agency-oriented urban production, and a key element in the development of the modern economic system predicated on urban industrialism. Grammar and Jamieson were not under strict coercive pressures, like enslaved laborers on a plantation. Instead they were responding to generalized conditions with entrepreneurial creativity, seizing on social and economic opportunities and making them work.

The former role of merchants was also changing at the turn of the nineteenth century. Generally wealthier than the craftsmen, the merchants were more capable of using political and financial channels to define the terms of the pro-manufacturing discourse. With import trading down in the 1790s, many merchants were busy collecting on old debts to keep up their income and finding creative things to do with their money. Some merchants reinvented themselves as merchant-manufacturers, investing in production industries and supply networks, and sometimes opening retail stores to sell their end products. These new merchant-manufacturers redefined production with technology, and they were capable of raising the money to finance them (Peskin 2003). In Annapolis, the merchant John Muir had been occupying himself through the 1790s lending his capital privately. By 1804 he decided that it would make more sense to lend it publicly and established the Farmers Bank of Maryland (Papenfuse 1975). From such events we can begin to analyze the effects of entrepreneurial decision-making and assess what factors were determinants of change and which were permissive of the system.

HIRED LABOR AND COMPLEX ORGANIZATIONS

Bakers made decisions about products, but the main cost they could control in the business was labor, and some of the most important decisions made were about labor organization and the manufacturing process. After the Revolution, artisan craftsmen continued to create individualized products, and the expansion into larger workshops generally meant the addition of more human labor through apprenticeships, indentures, or slaves. Urban society was socially stratified, and becoming more so. There were new roles for merchants and craftsmen but also for the working class and slaves as well, mostly in the way labor was organized and managed. The growth of a business enterprise by adding labor kept product costs high. The shift toward capitalism sought to counteract the amount of labor necessary per product through mechanization and automation of production.

We don't have a lot of direct evidence of labor use in bakeries from this research. Historical documents regarding the use of indentures and slaves by Chalmers and Jamieson is hard to quantify. There is, however, enough indication of organizational changes over time to be fairly certain of the attitude and environment for urban labor management in the mid-nineteenth century.

Andrew Jamieson owned eighteen slaves in 1810, making him one of the largest slaveholders in the city of Alexandria. By the nineteenth century, enslaved African Americans in the Chesapeake region had largely replaced white indentured labor. In urban areas like Annapolis and Alexandria, a new system developed, which I have called *slave indentures*. It was a system where enslaved blacks were contracted for terms of five or ten years, similar to that of white indentures (McCormac 1904). By 1821, Andrew Jamieson's original bakery employed seven men and five boys, who were probably a mix of enslaved, indentured, and maybe apprenticed labor. An assessment of the Andrew Jamieson & Son Bakery from about 1820 described the business as "formerly a large business, but now very circumscribed." This was probably a reference to the limitations created by city laws, labor practices, supply networks, and competition. A bigger reorganization of business practices was needed, and labor was one of the biggest variables both for cost and productivity.

The first big organizational change in the production process was the elimination of the master craftsman (e.g., Dawley 1976). We saw the start of this with Frederick Grammar and Andrew Jamieson at the turn of the nineteenth century, but those men still worked to some extent alongside the people they hired. By the 1830s, that transition was gaining speed across most urban production activities, as investors were increasingly taking control of production from the hands of the artisan craftsmen. In 1832, Robert Jamieson built a bakery on Water Street (later renamed Lee Street) in Alexandria that used a steam engine to power machines that could stamp out crackers and cookies in large quantities. Jamieson had learned about baking from his father, but as the second generation he kept his role in the operation as an investor and owner. There is no reason to believe that he ever worked at the steam bakery himself other than as a business manager. The factory was probably operated by enslaved labor, and maybe apprentices. Although Jamieson products were sold locally, the factory was positioned to accommodate distant markets. Beyond supplying the shipping vessels of Alexandria with bread, Jamieson's crackers were traded back to England and other distant places for retail sale. As the second generation, Robert Jamieson had capitalized on his father's trade. The process of baking by that time had been completely removed from the master craftsman and focused on productive efficiency—high volumes of baked goods with as little human labor as possible.

The ownership of the means of production, such as owning facilities and tools, was a powerful advantage over those who rented. Robert Jamieson's 1832 steam bakery had the newest facilities money could buy. The issues he had to navigate for his new bakery were the limits of the cash economy and the practice of slavery. There was not a free labor market, and for decades into the 1800s there was no money to enable a free labor market. We don't know the precise makeup of the factory workers in Jamieson's steam bakery, but slavery was prominent in Alexandria in the 1830s and 1840s. Most industries sought to obtain productive efficiency through progressive division of labor tasks, and this was probably Jamieson's goal as well. The organization and hiring of labor is a power contract between manager and worker. Maintaining a large enslaved workforce in urban areas was probably more expensive, and had more inherent risks, than a smaller paid labor force. Presumably Jamieson wanted to move away from a reliance on enslaved labor, but he probably continued the system that his father had used of slave indentures, such as the ten-year contracts.

Robert Jamieson was primarily an investor and businessman. When he built the steam bakery he probably conceived it in terms of mechanized production and purchased labor power. Jamieson's factory operations had achieved the separation of the product from the producer. In contrast to an artisan craftsman, whose labor is self-motivated, Jamieson's bakery operated with *socially deployed* labor in the sense that he paid for labor time, and that time was then directed toward specific activities. He was purchasing labor, but it was not fully commoditized labor in the capitalist sense. The slave indentures practiced by Jamieson's business were progressive for their time. Nevertheless, the labor organization at the bakery was the last holdover from the earlier neomercantile economy. Jamieson owned the bakery facilities and machines, and they were designed for mass production. He had found a way to resolve the labor needs of his bakery, and understood that a labor contract with incentives—such as freedom—benefitted both worker and employer. Methods of procuring labor to operate the factory had progressed to the point of individual contracts between employer and employed, but not within a free labor system.

These examples suggest the capitalist mode of production in the mid-Atlantic Chesapeake area arose by and large from self-enlightened economic interests of different social classes accommodating each other and a changing economy. On American plantations, power relationships were direct and personal. The relationships were clearly divided between the landholding elites and the poor landless laborers, a division that was often based on racial differences (Delle 1998; Singleton 1985). The urban manufacturing system was

different. It was a self-motivated market, in the economic sense. It was dominated more by the interests of capital wealth, and less by the moral paradigm
of equal rights. In Annapolis and Alexandria, however, it was somewhat in-
between. The merchants and managers who took over manufacturing were
the inheritors of the Georgian social principles of increasing individualism
(Leone 2005). This new urban production system seems to have benefitted enslaved African Americans to a degree, in that they had more opportunities for
freedom than those on plantations. The development of a free labor system
would be the final step in the incremental development of capitalism.

Factory production of any scale could not have existed in the Chesapeake
region much earlier than the 1832 steam bakery. The transition to a cash-
based economy in the United States was "slow and halting" (Henretta
1998:295). Common acceptance of a medium of currency, the U.S. dollar, and
the base of its value, were not complete in many places until the 1850s. In the
intervening years, the situation was complex. The increased availability of machinery allowed for profitability without labor increases, but it required investments. Jamieson's bakery appears to have led the way, mechanizing when
it was first technologically feasible, and well in advance of the abolition of
slavery. Jamieson probably built the steam bakery for reasons related to the
economic environment in Alexandria and the competitive bakery market. Developments in city infrastructure, such as municipal water supplies, also allowed for increases in the scale of production without substantial labor or
investment increase.

EFFECTS OF FINANCE AND BANKING

The financing institutions were important underwriters of all of the economic
developments discussed here, and developments in the financing sector can be
linked to most of the major changes. Chesapeake economics is closely linked
to Scottish economics, not only the large-scale kind of Adam Smith and
worldwide trade but also the smaller system of transactions, credit, and community capital. Small community exchange patterns were the norm in colonial days. In urban settings, credit and exchange predominated, and much of
the urban financial system was based on interpersonal relationships. In the
decades before the Revolution, America had a market economy that was expanding rapidly. A system had developed in which community exchange patterns were the norm. Extensive amounts of sumptuary goods were being

imported by merchants who relied on capital investment from Glasgow and the extension of credit by Scottish merchants such as Glassford & Company. This market, or mercantile, economy was more mature than the previous subsistence-plus system. However, it revolved around elements of earlier economic systems, including credit and barter, that operated differently in various local settings. As a result, the Revolutionary War era, and for some time afterwards, experienced an "immature state of American financial institutions and instruments" (Henretta 1998:304).

Different industries were prone to certain levels of investment, as well as to economic creativity. Some industries, like shoemaking, were known to have a *putting-out* system, where merchants provided cash advances and raw materials to the artisan craftsmen. When the products were completed, the merchants resold them at markup and took the profits (e.g., Commons 1909; Dawley 1976; Wolf 1982). There was no putting-out system for the baking industry, but I describe it here as a representative example of the creative financing schemes utilized in the precapitalist period.

After the Revolution, new local financial institutions and banks developed, along with new financial instruments such as American securities and bills of exchange. The American monetary system was established and began to function by the turn of the nineteenth century, at least in principle. Banks regularized payment schedules and relied on investment margins for their profits. Despite this, the cash economy took decades to become truly functional. Andrew Jamieson and Frederick Grammar had conducted their businesses in previous eras within a sort of kin-ordered economy. Relationships such as family and neighborhood ties were exploited at pivotal times to cover each others' debt collateral or for a ready loan. Glassford's stores had a similar way of offsetting payments through extended credit or creative exchange. The process leant itself to independence.

In the nineteenth century, urban businesses had to rely on actual loans and increasingly needed investors to achieve a viable scale of production. The new businesses were founded with monetary capital and were committed to growth as a means of staying competitive and maintaining investment margins. With a cash economy in effect and the capitalist mode of production, most of the vestiges of localized production dissolved. The financial alliances necessary to make a business successful precluded small-scale production and exchange of most common products, including the household bakery. This capitalization was one of the key changes to take place, and coincided with the change to an American economy separate from that of Europe.

PUBLIC FIRES

This book has suggested that arson was a criminal tool in the transition to capitalist manufacturing. Richard Fleming's bakery in Annapolis burned January 21, 1790, and Andrew Jamieson's bakery in Alexandria burned June 25, 1795. It is hypothesized here as more than a coincidence that these businesses, of the same type, burned at approximately the same time, and during a major economic transition. Answers to why this happened, who was involved, and what the motivations might have been extend across all the topics that this book has explored.

The most direct implication is that the merchants were behind the fires. Merchants made a significant income from imports and trade prior to the Revolutionary War. After the war, there was a domestic need for many products and a national interest in ramping up local production. The merchants who had lost trading business as a result of the war may have wanted to get into the production end of the retail cycle without having to compete with an established town craftsman. Additionally, it could be argued that urban business interests in general wanted to see the parochialism of the craftsman replaced with modernity.

Both the Fleming and Jamieson fires could likewise have resulted from personal grudges. In Annapolis, Fleming was involved in some questionable deals. He owed money to a con man, and was apparently beaten up right at, or right after, the time of the fire. It was an awkward situation in which Fleming may have been the victim, but potentially a situation in which he was somehow an accomplice. In Alexandria, Jamieson had standing grudges against both millers and city officials. He had published public challenges against some of these individuals, and readily participated in public petitions to increase regulation of the flour industry. Jamieson's stance could have angered the millers, or those who shipped the flour, or even the wheat growers.

Another explanation for the fires could be that, under the strains of a weak economy in the 1790s, both bakers set fire to their own shops in order to start anew without debts or other obligations. This seems unlikely for Fleming; the fire at Fleming's bakery was actually detrimental to him. Andrew Jamieson emerged from the fire at his bakery stronger than ever. More research may—or may not—reveal other motivations and evidence to address these events.

FINAL THOUGHTS

When did the Chesapeake area have capitalism? The transition from the eighteenth to nineteenth century saw many changes in American culture. Many of those themes have been followed in this book, including the ownership of production, the organization and tenure of labor, and the structure of manufacturing workshops. Most overlap each other, and in some cases are clearly interrelated. All are linked back to changes in the economic system, and more specifically to how processes of production were organized. The transitional stages of socioeconomic development from colonial craftsmen to industrialization give a nuanced perspective on the processes of economic growth and change toward capitalism. The story is basically the rise of American cities, involving a nexus of manufacturing knowledge, economic activity, investment capital, and a pool of labor that transformed raw materials into products for commercial consumption at the local and international scale.

The organizational practices associated with the bakery businesses document key stages of growth from small-scale household production to slightly larger-scale production, then to mechanized factory production. These data show changes in the baking industry that were small but substantial steps toward the emergence of a capitalist mode of production in the United States. We can see where different stages of production coincide with different economic structures, like the divisions and growth of management and labor sectors, changes in craftsmanship and its scale, and the roles of immigrant communities, financing institutions, urban development, and burgeoning technology.

This book has tried to avoid economic determinism and instead focus more holistically on the changing social relations of production that accompanied economic transformations. Over time there was a major restructuring of the relationships between manufacturing, money, markets, and power. Those social interactions are the processes that make up our daily lives. Communities, individuals, and households participate in distinct networks, or economic communities, based on unique variables such as family inheritances, landholdings, gender composition, or individual desires for wealth and status. Applying economic models toward understanding community processes is one way to understand a diversity of activities from a common perspective.

There was indeed a *great transformation* in the Chesapeake region in which the agrarian mode of production of the mid-1700s evolved into a capitalist manufacturing economy by the 1840s or 1850s. It was the cities and towns of the region, the locations where most manufacturing took place, that led the process. Some researchers see the effects primarily as negative, leading to disruption of family life, the breakdown of neighborhoods, and a deterioration of craft standards (e.g., Polanyi 1944). This research has tried to contextualize each change in the process, and has found, for the most part, that they were reactions made by choice, largely in response to global economic trends but also to localized social situations. Certain individuals, particularly middle-class artisan craftsmen, were in a position to respond to opportunities and make changes to their businesses. Baking was largely capitalized by 1832 in terms of factory production, using purchased labor that was removed from the skilled craftsman. The final step to capitalism, a free wage labor system, would still be three decades away in the Chesapeake tidewater region and required a Civil War to fully implement.

Appendix
Emancipation in the United States

The following is a letter from "A VIRGINIAN (a.k.a. Samuel Janney), Virginia, December 9, 1844," published in the *Alexandria Gazette and Virginia Advertiser*, December 11, 1844:

■ ■ ■

In a late number of the *Alexandria Gazette*, my attention was called, by some editorial remarks, to a plan proposed by M. B. Sampson for emancipation of the Slaves in the United States. This is a matter of such deep interest to all the citizens of the Slave-holding States, that, I suppose, there are few among us who do not at time reflect upon it; but unhappily it has for many years been considered almost an interdicted subject, and but little discussion has been allowed, except on the part of those who have been disposed to apologies for an acknowledged evil, by charging it upon the Government of Great Britain, which, before the revolution, refused to prohibit the introduction of Slaves into the American Colonies.

In order to illustrate the policy we are pursuing in relation to this question, the territory of the old Slave-holding States, may be compared to a landed estate, which an indolent proprietor has inherited from his ancestors. The soil is naturally good, but has been exhausted by injudicious cultivation; the buildings originally commodious, are going to decay; the mineral riches which are known to be great are unproductive; the water power is abundant, but only a small portion of it rendered available, and the roads leading through the estate are in a wrenched condition. All these evils spring from one grand defect in the management of the estate, which was adopted in a former age, and has been continued by each succeeding generation, down to the present day. This defect consists in the employment of laborers having no interest in the products of the soil, and without skill or knowledge to develop the resources of the estate.

Some years ago, the owners of this property became conscious that a radical change in the system of management was necessary, and talked openly, and earnestly, of what ought to be done; but about that time it happened that some of his neighbors, who had adopted a better system, and were growing rich, began to advise him to follow their example, and to insist that it ought to be done immediately, as every hour's delay increased the evil, and made the remedy more difficult. What! Says the chivalric old gentleman, do you presume to advise me in the management of my own property? Am I not pursuing the same course that was adopted by my patriotic ancestors? If the estate is becoming exhausted, the buildings going to decay, and the tenants leaving it in despair, that is none of your business. The burdens under which I am laboring, are not of my imposing,—they were entailed upon the estate by my forefathers, and I am not responsible for them.

Such is substantially the course pursued by the people of the Southern States in relation to the institution of Slavery. Instead of examining this important question with close attention, discussing it among ourselves with manly independence, and seeking from the experience of others, all the light we can obtain, many of our citizens seem to consider it a question too delicate to be meddled with, and willfully shut their eyes upon the dangers that surround us. The last census disclosed the alarming fact that the population of Eastern Virginia, had in ten years been diminished twenty six thousand inhabitants, and the process of depopulation is still going on with increased rapidity. I have seen it stated on good authority that a large estate was lately sold in Sussex County, for one dollar to one dollar and a quarter per acre. It is well-known to all who have traveled in the South-eastern part of the State, that large tracts which were formerly cultivated, are now covered with forests; insomuch that deer and other game are becoming more abundant in some places than they have been at any period since the settlement of the country.

In an address lately delivered before the New Castle (Del.) Agricultural Society, the attention of the audience was called to the fact that land may be had in Virginia, at from 20 cents to $5 per acre, and the advantage of a settlement in this State, were stated to be greatly superior to any that are afforded by the Western States or Territories. We see frequent appeals in the Virginia papers, addressed to the Northern people to come and fill up our waste places and lend us the invigorating influence of their industrious habits, and skillful management. About fifty such families have settled in Fairfax County, and the effect of their labors is already visible upon the face of the country. They have erected many neat dwellings, reclaimed a considerable extent of exhausted land, and given a spur to industry and enterprise, that has improved the value of real estate all around them. On making inquiry lately of one of their neighbors, who is deeply interested in the success of their experiment, he informed me, that those among them who had purchased land seemed satisfied with their prospects, but the young men who had come with them from the North, as laborers had mostly gone back. This is much to be regretted, but a different result could hardly have been expected, while they are surrounded by slave laborers. The inevitable result of slavery is to degrade labor in the estimation of the people, and men who have been brought up in free States, where the laborer is treated with respect and feels his independence, cannot brook to be looked down upon by the idle drones who infest all Slave-holding communities. There is not the least possibility of such a population from the North, being induced to settle in the lower part of the State, where they are most needed, unless something be done to assure them that slavery with its desolating influences will be done away. That it might be removed without danger, and with great benefit to all classes, I have not a shadow of doubt; but in order to effect this we must be willing to discuss it calmly, and to examine with attention the results which have taken place in other States, where the transition has actually taken place.

The Paris papers announce that France is taking steps to abolish Negro Slavery in her Colonies. The Government of Denmark, has some time since built school-houses throughout her West Indies Islands, to which the young slaves are required to be sent in order to prepare them for Emancipation,— and in Portugal a bill has lately been introduced into the Chamber of Peers, for the abolition of slavery in their East India possessions, which although it was lost by a vote of 23 to 18, shows that the subject begins to be agitated even in that benighted kingdom. Shall we then who profess the most ardent devotion to liberty remain inactive and indifferent while the whole Christian world is becoming awakened to a conviction of that great truth first proclaimed by our fathers, that life, liberty, and the pursuit of happiness, are the inalienable birthright of man? The question of compensation is the only one that presents any real difficulty; but even this it appears to me, might be settled, if it could be dispassionately considered with a sincere desire to do the best in our power. Many years ago a proposition was made by Rufus King, of New York, in the senate of the U.S., to appropriate the proceeds of the public lands to the extinguishments of slavery; and, although the movement was then denounced by Southern politicians as an indication of disposition to interfere with Southern rights, I believe that many judicious men would now view it in a very different light. During the memorable debate on slavery, in the legislature of Virginia, in 1832, General Brodnax alluded to this proposition in the following language: "Whatever political heresies Rufus King may have committed, I, for one, regard this as a redeeming act of his life. Should no other member do so, it is my intention, at a proper time, to offer resolutions instructing our Senators, and requesting our Representatives, in Congress, to propose the amendment to the Constitution, which may be necessary to authorize this disbursement of the federal funds." This proposition appears to me much more eligible than the one proposed by M. B. Sampson, to which I could point out great objections.

I will now propose a few queries which have been suggested by reading several well attested accounts of the results of emancipation in the British West Indies.

1st. If emancipation without removal would be a dangerous measure in the United States, how shall we account for the fact, that in Antigua and other British Islands, where the slaves formed a much larger proportion of the population, no injury has resulted, but on the contrary, great benefits to all classes.

2nd. If the removal of our colored population would be desirable, what can be the reason that the authorities of Barbadoes, since emancipation, have endeavored to prevent their colored laborers from emigrating.

3rd. As the free colored people who have gone from the United States to Trinidad, are found to be a useful and industrious class, and the planters are desirous to obtain more of them, is it not probable they would be equally useful here, if protected by humane laws, and encouraged by the education of their children.

4th. Would not the colonization of the colored race, without their consent, be equivalent to their expulsion; and can such a measure be justified on Christian principles? Would it not be as disgraceful as the banishment of the Huguenots from France, the expulsion of the Jews from Spain, or the exile of the patriotic Poles?

5th. Is it not safe in all cases to act upon the principle taken for the motto of the *Alexandria Gazette?*—"Fait ce qu'il faut, arrive ce qu'il pourra."

Bibliography

Abell, Julie D., and Petar D. Glumac. 1997. Beneath the MCI Center: Insight into Washington's historic water supply. *Washington History* 9 (1):25–41.

Alexandria Husting's Court. 1799. Plat of lots on new land east of old lot 31. Husting's Court Book L [1799], p. 362.

American Anti-Slavery Society. 1836. *Anti-slavery broadside*. New York: Author.

Artemel, Janice G., Elizabeth A. Crowell, and J. Parker. 1987. *The Alexandria slave pen: The archaeology of urban captivity*. Report prepared by Engineering-Science.

Baker, Alfred Cookman. 1899. *History of state banking in Maryland*. Baltimore, Md.: John Hopkins University Press.

Baker, Nancy. 1986. Annapolis, Maryland 1695–1730. *Maryland Historical Magazine* 81:191–209.

Barr, Keith L., Pamela J. Cressey, and Barbara H. Magid. 1994. How sweet it was: Alexandria's sugar trade and refining business. In *Historical archaeology of the Chesapeake*, ed. Paul A. Shackel and Barbara J. Little, 251–65. Washington, D.C.: Smithsonian Institution.

Ben-Atar, Doron. 1995. Alexander Hamilton's alternative: Technology piracy and the report on manufactures. *William and Mary Quarterly*, 3rd series, 52 (3):389–414.

Blaszczyk, Regina Lee. 1984. Ceramics and the sot-weed factor: The china market in a tobacco economy. *Winterthur Portfolio* 19 (1):7–19.

Bowling, Kenneth R. 1988. *Creating the federal city, 1774–1800: Potomac fever.* Washington, D.C.: American Institute of Architects.

Braudel, Fernand. 1979. *Civilization and capitalism—15th–18th centuries, volume II: The wheels of commerce.* New York: Harper and Row.

Breen, Timothy H. 2004. *The marketplace of revolution: How consumer politics shaped American independence.* New York: Oxford University Press.

Bridenbaugh, Carl. 1950. *Colonial craftsmen.* Chicago: University of Chicago Press.

Brugger, Robert J. 1988. *Maryland, a middle temperament, 1634–1980.* Baltimore, Md.: Johns Hopkins University Press.

Buckeye Engine Company. 1849. Thompson's automatic governor cut-off engine. Manufactured exclusively by the Buckeye Engine Company, Salem, Columbiana Co., Ohio. Placard in Library of Congress American memory series, An American time capsule: Three centuries of broadsides and other printed ephemera. Portfolio 138, Folder 31. At hdl.loc.gov/loc.rbc/rbpe.13803100.

Carson, Cary, Norman F. Barka, William M. Kelso, Garry Wheeler Stone, and Dell Upton. 1981. Impermanent architecture in the southern American colonies. *Winterthur Portfolio* 16 (2/3):135–96.

Chayanov, A. V. 1966. *The theory of peasant economy,* ed. D. Thorner, B. Kerblay, and R. E. F. Smith. Illinois: Blackwell.

Commons, John R. 1909. American shoemakers, 1648–1895: A sketch of industrial evolution. *Quarterly Journal of Economics* 24 (1):39–84.

Cooke, Ebenezer. 1707. *The sot-weed factor; or a voyage to Maryland, a satyr.* Originally published in London.

Coulter Jr., Calvin Brewster. 1944. *The Virginia merchant.* Ph.D. diss., Princeton University.

Crothers, Glenn A. 2005. Quaker merchants and slavery in early national Alexandria, Virginia: The ordeal of William Hartshorne. *Journal of the Early Republic* 25 (1):47–77

Crutchfield, Parker. 1953. *Bakers and baking in 18th century America, with a brief sketch of their old world beginnings and the same among the earliest English colonists in America.* Williamsburg, Va.: Colonial Williamsburg Foundation.

Cuddy, Thomas W., Francine W. Bromberg, Heather Crowl, T. Michael Miller, Kevin Mock, and Cynthia Pfanstiel. 2006. *The North Lee Street project: A phase I, II, and III archaeological investigation.* Technical report. Gaithersburg, Md. and Alexandria, Va.: URS Corporation and Alexandria Archaeology.

Cuddy, Thomas W., and Mark P. Leone. 2008. New Africa: Understanding the Americanization of African descent groups through archaeology. In *Collaboration in archaeological practice: Engaging descendant communities,* ed. Chip Colwell-Chanthaphonh and T. J. Ferguson. Lanham, Md.: AltaMira.

Cuddy, Thomas W., and Jason P. Shellenhamer. 2005. *Phase III archaeological excavations at 99 Main Street, 18AP21, Annapolis, Maryland.* Excavation report for Historic Annapolis Foundation. Gaithersburg, Md.: URS Corporation.

Daniels, Christine. 1993. "Wanted—A blacksmith who understands plantation work": Artisans in Maryland, 1700–1810. *William and Mary Quarterly,* 3rd series, 50 (4):743–67.

Dawley, Alan. 1976. *Class and community: The Industrial Revolution in Lynn.* Cambridge, Mass.: Harvard University Press.

Deetz, James. 1977. *In small things forgotten: The archaeology of early America.* New York: Anchor Press.

———. 1988. Material culture and worldview in colonial Anglo-America. In *The recovery of meaning: Historical archaeology in the eastern United States,* ed. Mark P. Leone and Parker B. Potter, Jr., 219–33. Washington, D.C.: Smithsonian Institution.

Deines, Ann. 1994. *The slave population in 1810 Alexandria, Virginia: A preservation plan for historic resources.* Master's thesis, George Washington University.

DeLeuw, Cather, & Company. 1999. *Data recovery excavations at site 44PW855, town of Dumfries, Prince William County, Virginia, U.S. Route 1/Possum Point Road.* Excavation report for the Virginia Department of Transportation. Fairfax, Va.: DeLeuw Cather & Co.

Delle, James A. 1998. *An archaeology of social space: Analyzing coffee plantations in Jamaica's Blue Mountains.* New York: Plenum.

Dennee, Timothy J. 2001. *Slave manumissions in Alexandria land records, 1791–1863.* At www.freedmenscemetery.org/Dennee_Pages/slave_manumissions_in_alexandria.htm, accessed March 23, 2005.

Devine, Thomas Martin. 1990. *The tobacco lords: A study of the tobacco merchants of Glasgow and their trading activities, c. 1740–90*. Edinburgh, Scotland: Edinburgh University Press.

Duclow, Geraldine. 1989. Christopher Ludwig: The gingerbread patriot. *Germantown Crier* 41 (4):77–80.

Duffy, Thomas F. 1965. *The decline of the port of Alexandria, Virginia, 1800–1861*. Master's thesis, Georgetown University. Copy on file at the Alexandria Library Special Collections.

Durrenberger, E. P., ed. 1984. *Chayanov, peasants and economic anthropology*. Orlando, Fla.: Academic.

Ernst, Howard R. 2003. *Chesapeake Bay blues: Science, politics, and the struggle to save the bay*. Lanham, Md.: Rowman & Littlefield.

Ernst, Joseph. 1973. *Money and politics in America, 1755–1775*. Chapel Hill: University of North Carolina Press.

Ewing, Maskell C. 1845. *Plan of the town of Alexandria, D.C. with the environs*. Philadelphia: T. Sinclair.

Fergusson, Robert. n.d. *Robert Fergusson papers*. Special Collections, Georgetown University Libraries. Finding aid available at www.library.georgetown.edu/dept/speccoll/cl263.htm.

Fischler, Benjamin R., G. Gwiazda, S. Lewthwaite, and J. P. McCarthy. 1999. *Phase I archeological investigation of the proposed construction area for New Piscataway Road north of Floral Park Road (MD Route 223—Floral Park Road and Piscataway Road—Milepost 0.63), proposed greens at Piscataway development, Prince George's County, Maryland*. Report prepared for Greenvest, L.C. Greenbelt, Md.: Greenhorne & O'Mara.

Flannery, Kent V., ed. 1976. *The early Mesoamerican village*. San Diego, Calif.: Academic.

Fry, Joshua, and Peter Jefferson. 1755. *Map of the most inhabited parts of Virginia, containing the whole province of Maryland with part of Pensilvania, New Jersey and North Carolina*. Reproduction of 1752 original. Courtesy of the Library of Congress.

Furgerson, Kathleen A., Varna G. Boyd, Thomas W. Cuddy, and Cassandra Michaud. 2005. *Phase III archaeological data recovery, sites 18PR479, 18PR478, 18PR482, and*

18PR496, preserve at Piscataway, Prince George's County, Maryland. Report for Bailey's Associates. Gaithersburg, Md.: URS Corporation.

Galenson, David. 1981. *White servitude in colonial America: An economic analysis.* New York: Cambridge University Press.

Gibb, James G. 1996. *The archaeology of wealth: Consumer behavior in English America.* New York: Plenum.

Goodwin, R. Christopher and Associates. 1993. *Phase II/III archeological investigations of the Gott's Court parking facility, Annapolis, Maryland, Vol. I and II.* Report for the city of Annapolis. Washington, D.C.: R. Christopher Goodwin & Associates.

Green, George D. 1972. Louisiana 1804–1861. In *Banking and economic development: Some lessons of history,* ed. Rondo Cameron, 199–231. London: Oxford University Press.

Hardy, Stephen Gregg. 1999. *Trade and economic growth in the eighteenth century Chesapeake.* Ph.D. dissertation, University of Maryland at College Park.

Harlen, Christine Margerum. 1999. A reappraisal of classical economic nationalism and economic liberalism. *International Studies Quarterly* 43 (4):733–44.

Henderson, Alexander. 1999. *Virginia merchants : Alexander Henderson, factor for John Glassford at his Colchester store, Fairfax County, Virginia, his letter book of 1758–1765.* Transcribed and ed. Charles and Virginia Hamrick. Athens, Ga.: Iberian Publishing.

Henretta, James A. 1998. The "market" in the early republic. *Journal of the Early Republic* 18 (2):289–304.

Hickin, Patricia. 1971. Gentle agitator: Samuel M. Janney and the antislavery movement in Virginia, 1842–1851. *Journal of Southern History* 37 (2):159–90.

Historic St. Mary's City. 2004. Rebuilding the brick chapel of 1667. At www.stmaryscity.org/ChapelProgress/Bricks.html, accessed December 28, 2004.

Hollander, Jacob. 1927. Adam Smith, 1776–1926. *Journal of Political Economy* 35 (2):153–97.

Hurst, Harold W. 1991. *Alexandria on the Potomac: Portrait of an antebellum community.* Lanham, Md.: University Press of America.

Jernegan, Marcus. 1978. Slavery and the beginnings of industrialism in the American colonies. In *The other slaves: Mechanics, artisans, and craftsmen,* ed. James E. Newton and Randall L. Lewis, 3–20. Boston: G. K. Hall.

John Glassford & Company. n.d. A register of its records. Library of Congress Manuscript Division. At lcweb2.loc.gov/cgi-bin/query/r?faid/faid: @field(DOCID+ms998016), accessed January 2005.

Johnson, Matthew. 1996. *An archaeology of capitalism.* New York: Blackwell.

Kellock, Katherine A. 1962. *Colonial Piscataway in Maryland.* Accokeek, Md.: Alice Ferguson Foundation.

Kelso, William M. 1984. *Kingsmill Plantations, 1619–1800: Archaeology and country life in colonial Virginia.* Charlottesville: University of Virginia Press.

Kulikoff, Allan. 1979. Economic growth in the eighteenth-century Chesapeake. *Journal of Economic History* 39 (1979): 275–88.

———. 1986. *Tobacco and slaves: The development of southern cultures in the Chesapeake, 1680–1800.* Chapel Hill: University of North Carolina Press.

———. 1993. Households and markets: Towards a new synthesis of American agrarian history. *William and Mary Quarterly* 50 (2):342–55.

———. 2000. *From British peasants to colonial American farmers.* Chapel Hill: University of North Carolina Press.

Leone, Mark P. 1984. Interpreting ideology in historical archaeology: Using the rules of perspective in the William Paca garden, Annapolis, Maryland. In *Ideology, power, and prehistory,* ed. Daniel Miller and Christopher Tilley, pp. 25–36. New York: Cambridge University Press.

———. 1988. The Georgian order as the order of merchant capitalism in Annapolis, Maryland. In *The recovery of meaning: Historical archaeology in the eastern United States,* ed. Mark P. Leone and Parker B. Potter, Jr., 235–61. Washington, D.C.: Smithsonian Institution.

———. 1995. A historic archaeology of capitalism. *American Anthropologist* 97 (2 June):251–68.

———. 2005. *The archaeology of liberty in an American capital: Excavations in Annapolis.* Berkeley: University of California Press.

Leone, Mark P., Jennifer A. Stabler, and Anna-Marie Burlaga. 1998. A street plan for hierarchy in Annapolis: An analysis of State Circle as a geometric form. In

Annapolis pasts: Historical archaeology in Annapolis, Maryland, ed. Paul A. Shackel, Paul R. Mullins, and Mark S. Warner, 291–306. Knoxville: University of Tennessee Press.

Letzer, Mark, and Jean B. Russo. 2003. *The diary of William Faris, 1792–1804: The daily life of an Annapolis silversmith.* Baltimore: Maryland Historical Society.

Licht, Walter. 1995. *Industrializing America: The nineteenth century.* Baltimore: Johns Hopkins University Press.

Lindauer, Anthony D. 1997. *From paths to plats: The development of Annapolis, 1651 to 1718.* Annapolis: Maryland State Archives and the Maryland Historical Trust.

Little, Barbara J. 1994. "She was . . . an example to her sex": Possibilities for a feminist historical archaeology. In *The historical archaeology of the Chesapeake*, ed. Paul A. Shackel and Barbara J. Little, 189–204. Washington, D.C.: Smithsonian Institution.

Luckenbach, Al. 1995. *Providence 1649: The history and archaeology of Anne Arundel County, Maryland's first European settlement.* Maryland State Archives and the Maryland Historical Trust Studies in Local History. Annapolis: Whitmore Printing Company.

Mack, Ann H. 1987. John Glassford and Company of Virginia and Maryland: Purchasers at the Dumfries store. *Virginia Genealogist* 31 (2):122–30.

Macoll, John D., and George J. Stansfield, eds. 1977. *Alexandria: A town in transition, 1800–1900.* Alexandria, Va.: Alexandria Historical Society.

Martenet, Simon J. 1861. Prince George's County District No. 5, Piscataway. *Martenet's Atlas of Maryland*, Library of Congress.

Marx, Karl. [1867] 1990. *Capital, volume 1: A critique of political economy.* New York: Penguin.

Maryland State Archives. n.d. At www.msa.md.gov.

Matthews, Christopher N. 2001. Political economy and race: Comparative archaeologies of Annapolis and New Orleans in the eighteenth century. In *Race and the archaeology of identity*, ed. Charles E. Orser, Jr., 71–87. Salt Lake City: University of Utah Press.

Matthews, Peter, transcriber. 1988. *Alexandria (D.C.) directory: 1834 occupational listing.* Excerpt for the county and city of Alexandria, office of Historic Alexandria.

McCarney, Scott. 1998. *Plates from Diderot/Doubleday/Deconstruction: Images of tradesmen and women in the book arts as depicted in L'Encyclopedie ou Dictionnaire Raisonne des Sciences, des Art et des Metiers of Denis Diderot.* Original Diderot publication 1751. Rochester, N.Y.: Doubleday.

McCormac, Eugene Irving. 1904. *White servitude in Maryland, 1634–1820.* Studies in Historical and Political Science, XXII, Nos. 3–4. Baltimore: Johns Hopkins University Press.

McCusker, John J., and Russell R. Menard. 1985. *The economy of British America, 1607–1789.* Chapel Hill: University of North Carolina Press.

McIntire, Robert Harry. 1980. *Genealogies of Annapolis families.* At www.rootsweb.com/~mdannear/mcintire.htm, accessed March 2008.

McKnight, Justine Woodward. 2005. 99 Main Street, Annapolis (site 18AP21) wood identification. In *Phase III archaeological excavations at 99 Main Street, 18AP21, Annapolis, Maryland,* ed. Thomas W. Cuddy and Jason P. Shellenhamer. Report for the Historic Annapolis Foundation. Gaithersburg, Md.: URS Corporation.

Means, Bernard K., ed. 1999. *A guide to artifacts from the Lee Street site.* Alexandria Archaeology publication No. 105. Alexandria: Office of Historic Alexandria, Virginia.

Merrill, Michael. 1995. Putting capitalism in its place. *William and Mary Quarterly* 52:315–26.

Merchants of Alexandria. 1922. Inspection of wheat. Petition of the merchants of Alexandria, October 19, 1787, to the Honorable House of Delegates of Virginia. Reprinted in *William and Mary Quarterly,* 2nd Series, Vol. 2:288–91.

———. 1923. Petition of the merchants of Alexandria, October 9, 1792, to the Honorable General Assembly of Virginia. Reprinted in *William and Mary Quarterly,* 2nd Series, Vol. 3:206–8.

Middleton, Arthur Pierce. [1953] 1984. *Tobacco coast, a maritime history of the Chesapeake Bay in the colonial period.* Baltimore: Johns Hopkins University Press.

Middleton, Simon. 2001. "How it came that the bakers bake no bread": A struggle for trade privileges in seventeenth-century New Amsterdam. *William and Mary Quarterly* 58 (2):347–72.

Miller, George L. 2000. Telling time for archaeologists. *Northeast Historical Archaeology* 29:1–22.

Miller, T. Michael. 1987. *Pen portraits of Alexandria, Virginia, 1739–1900*. Bowie, Md: Heritage.

———. 1991. *Artisans & merchants of Alexandria, Virginia, 1780–1820*. Vol. I. Bowie, Md.: Heritage.

———. 1992a. *Alexandria city officialdom, 1749–1992*. Bowie, Md.: Heritage.

———. 1992b. *Artisans & merchants of Alexandria, Virginia, 1780–1820*. Vol. II. Bowie, Md.: Heritage.

———. 1995. *Portrait of a town: Alexandria*. Bowie, Md.: Heritage.

———. 1997. An overview of the Jamieson/Hill Steam Bakery. In *Moments in Time: Alexandria Archaeology Volunteer News* XV(11).

———, compiler. 1998. *"Crackers for the Queen"—A history of the block bounded by Thompson's Alley, Lee, Queen and Union Streets*. Unpublished manuscript, on file at the Alexandria Archaeology Laboratory, Torpedo Factory, Alexandria, Va.

———. n.d. *Steam engines and their use in nineteenth century Alexandria, Virginia*. Unpublished manuscript, on file at the Alexandria Archaeology Laboratory, Torpedo Factory, Alexandria, Va.

Moser, Jason D., Al Luckenbach, Sherri M. Marsh, and Donna Ware. 2003. Impermanent architecture in a less permanent town: The mid-seventeenth-century architecture of Providence, Maryland. *Perspectives in vernacular architecture* 9 (Constructing image, identity, and place):197–214.

Moss, James E. 1976. *Providence: Ye lost towne at Severn*. Baltimore: Maryland Historical Society.

Mumford, Willard R. 2002. *Barter, bits, bills, and tobacco: The story of money in early Maryland*. Annapolis: Maryland State Archives and the Maryland Historical Trust.

———. 2005. More on the search for the Chalmers' Mint: A further analysis. . . . *The Anne Arundel County History Notes* XXXVI(2).

Newman, Henry W. [1940] 1971. *Charles County gentry: A genealogical history of six emigrants . . . and the descendents*. Reprint of the 1940 edition. Baltimore: Genealogical Publishing.

Newton, James E., and Randall L. Lewis. 1978. *The other slaves: Mechanics, artisans, and craftsmen*. Boston: G. K. Hall.

Noël Hume, Ivor. 1969a. *A guide to artifacts of colonial America*. New York: Vintage.

———. 1969b. *The wells of Williamsburg: Colonial time capsules*. Colonial Williamsburg Archaeological Series No. 4, Williamsburg, Va.

———. 1970. *James Geddy and sons, colonial craftsmen*. Colonial Williamsburg Archaeological Series No. 5, Williamsburg, Va.

The North Star. 1848. Slavery and Methodism. Volume I, Number XVI, page 1, April 14.

Orr, Kenneth G. 1975. *Preliminary field report on the archaeological excavation of the 99 Main Street Site, Annapolis, Maryland, November, 1974–February 1975*. Report on file at the Historic Annapolis Foundation Archaeology Laboratory and the Maryland Historical Trust.

Orser, Charles E., Jr. 1988. *Toward a theory of power for historical archaeology: Plantations and space*. In *The recovery of meaning: Historical archaeology in the eastern United States*, ed. Mark P. Leone and Parker B. Potter, Jr., 313–44. Washington, D.C.: Smithsonian Institution.

Outlaw, Merry Abbitt. 2002. Scratched in clay: Seventeenth-century North Devon slipware at Jamestown, Virginia. In *Ceramics in America*, ed. Robert Hunter, 17–38. London: Chipstone Foundation.

Owens, Christopher. 1973. Nomination to the National Register of Historic Places. Document prepared by the Maryland National Capital Parks and Planning Commission and submitted to Robert Arciprete, Prince George's Regional Office, April 27, 1973.

Papenfuse, Edward A. 1972. Planter behavior and economic opportunity in a staple economy. *Agricultural History*, April.

———. 1975. *In pursuit of profit*. Baltimore: Johns Hopkins University Press.

Papenfuse, Edward C., Gregory A. Stiverson, Alan F. Day, and David W. Jordan, eds. 1979. *A biographical dictionary of the Maryland Legislature, 1635–1789*. 2 Vols. Baltimore: Johns Hopkins University Press.

Paynter, Robert. 1988. Steps to an archaeology of capitalism. In *The recovery of meaning: Historical archaeology in the eastern United States*, ed. Mark P. Leone and Parker B. Potter, Jr., 407–33. Washington, D.C.: Smithsonian Institution.

Pearl, S., M. King, and H. S. Berger. 1991. *Historic contexts in Prince George's County: Short papers on settlement patterns, transportation and cultural history*. Upper Marlboro, Md.: Prince George's County Planning Department.

Pearson, Marlys J. 1991. *Archaeological excavations at 18AP14: The Victualling Warehouse site, 77 Main Street, Annapolis, Maryland, 1982–84*. Report on file at the Historic Annapolis Foundation Archaeological Laboratory and the Maryland Historical Trust.

Perge, C. 1980. *A historical survey of Alexandria's water supply, 1755–1852*. Unpublished essay, on file at Alexandria Archaeology, Alexandria, Va.

Perkins, Edwin J. 1980. *The economy of colonial America*. New York: Columbia University Press.

Peskin, Lawrence A. 2003. *Manufacturing revolution: The intellectual origins of early American industry*. Baltimore: Johns Hopkins University Press.

Philadelphia Inquirer. 1863. Article regarding the Union Army Headquarters in Alexandria during the Civil War. August 8.

Pippenger, Wesley E. 1995. *Legislative petitions of the town of Alexandria, Virginia, 1778–1861*. Westminster, Md.: Family Line.

———. 2001. *Husbands and wives associated with early Alexandria, Virginia and the surrounding area*. Westminster, Md.: Willow Bend.

Polanyi, Karl. 1944. *The great transformation: The political and economic origins of our time*. New York: Farrar and Reinhart.

———. 1957. The economy as instituted process. In *Trade and markets in early empires*, ed. Karl Polanyi, Conrad M. Arensberg, and Harry W. Pearson, 243–69. Glencoe, Ill.: Free Press.

Prattis, J. Iain. 1987. Alternative views of economy in economic anthropology. In *Beyond the new economic anthropology*, ed. John Clammer, 8–44. London: McMillan.

Preisser, Thomas M. 1977. *18th-century Alexandria, Virginia, before the Revolution, 1749–1776*. Ph.D. diss., College of William and Mary, Williamsburg, Va.

———. 1982. White servant labor in colonial Alexandria, 1749–1776. *Northern Virginia Heritage* IV (2):15–19.

Price, Jacob M. 1954. The rise of Glasgow in the Chesapeake tobacco trade, 1707–1775. *William and Mary Quarterly*, 3rd Series, 11 (2):179–99.

———. 1987. A revolution of scale in overseas trade: British firms in the Chesapeake trade 1675–1775. *Journal of Economic History* 47:1–43.

———. 1995. Merchants and planters: The market structure of the colonial Chesapeake reconsidered. In *Tobacco in the Atlantic trade: The Chesapeake, London, and Glasgow, 1675–1775*. 1–32. Aldershot, U.K.: Variorum.

Pritchett, Dylan. 1993. *A look at the African-American community through Alexandria's eyes: 1780–1810*. A report of the "For Preserving Alexandria's Cultural Traditions (PACT) Project, January, 1993." Alexandria Library Special Collections.

Reps, John W. 1972. *Tidewater towns: City planning in colonial Virginia and Maryland*. Williamsburg, Va.: Colonial Williamsburg Foundation.

Ridgely, David. 1841. *Annals of Annapolis*. Baltimore: Cushing and Brother.

Riley, Elihu S. 1887. *The ancient city: A history of Annapolis, in Maryland, 1649–1887*. Annapolis Record Printing Office.

———. 1901. *Annapolis . . . "Ye Ancient Capital of Maryland."* Annapolis, Md.: Annapolis Publishing.

Ring, Constance K., and Wesley E. Pippenger, compilers. 1995. *Alexandria, Virginia town lots, 1749–1801: Together with proceedings of the Board of Trustees, 1749–1780*. Westminster, Md.: Family Line.

Ripley, William Zebina. 1893. *The financial history of Virginia, 1609–1776*. Studies in History, Economics and Public Law, Vol. IV, No. 1. New York: Columbia College.

Rock, Howard B., Paul A. Gilje, and Robert Asher, eds. 1995. *American artisans: Crafting society identity, 1750–1850*. Baltimore: Johns Hopkins University Press.

Roseberry, William. 1988. Political economy. *Annual Review of Anthropology* 17:161–85.

Rothschild, Emma. 1992. Adam Smith and conservative economics. *The Economic History Review*, New Series, 45 (1):74–96.

Rothschild, Nan. 1990. *New York City neighborhoods: The eighteenth century*. New York: Academic.

Russo, Jean B. 1988. Self sufficiency and local exchange: Free craftsmen in the rural Chesapeake economy. In *Colonial Chesapeake society*, ed. Lois Green Carr, 389–432. Chapel Hill: University of North Carolina Press.

Sahlins, Marshall. 1972. *Stone Age economics*. New York: Aldine.

Schlesinger, Arthur Meir. 1957. *The colonial merchants and the American Revolution*. New York: Frederick Ungar.

Schoepf, Johann David. [1788] 2007. *Travels in the Confederation*. Whitefish, Mont.: Kessinger.

Sellers, Charles. 1994. *The market revolution: Jacksonian America, 1815–1846*. New York: Oxford University Press.

Shackel, Paul V. 1994. Town plans and everyday material culture: An archaeology of social relations in colonial Maryland's capital cities. In *Historical archaeology of the Chesapeake*, ed. Paul V. Shackel and Barbara J. Little, 85–96. Washington, D.C.: Smithsonian Institution.

Sharrer, G. Terry. 1977. Commerce and industry. In *Alexandria: A towne in transition, 1800–1900*, ed. John D. Macoll and George J. Stansfield. Alexandria, Va.: Alexandria Historical Society.

Shephard, Steven Judd. 1985. *An archaeological study of socioeconomic stratification: Status change in 19th century Alexandria, Virginia*. Ph.D. diss., Southern Illinois University.

———. 1988. *Obtaining water and discarding waste: An overview of attitudes and practices in nineteenth century Virginia*. Alexandria, Va.: Alexandria Archaeology.

Sherman, William. 2005. Examination of mortar samples from the excavations at 196 Green Street (18AP21). In *Phase III archaeological excavations at 99 Main Street, 18AP21, Annapolis, Maryland*, by Thomas W. Cuddy and Jason P. Shellenhamer. Report for the Historic Annapolis Foundation. Gaithersburg, Md.: URS Corporation.

Shomette, Donald. 1985. *Maritime Alexandria: An evaluation of submerged cultural resource potentials at Alexandria, Virginia*. Report prepared for Office of Historic Alexandria, Virginia.

Singleton, Theresa, ed. 1985. *The archaeology of slavery and plantation life*. New York: Academic.

Smith, Adam. [1776] 2000. *The wealth of nations*. Ed. Edwin Cannan. With intro. by Robert Reich. New York: Modern Library.

Smith, William Francis, and T. Michael Miller. 1989. *A seaport saga: Portrait of old Alexandria*. Norfolk, Va.: Donning.

Soltow, J. H. 1959. Scottish traders in Virginia, 1750–1775. *The Economic History Review*, New Series, 12 (1):83–98.

South, Stanley. 1977. *Method and theory in historical archaeology*. New York: Academic.

Spencer-Wood, Suzanne M., ed. 1987. *Consumer choice in historical archaeology*. New York: Plenum.

Sprouse, Edith Moore. 1975. *Colchester: Colonial port on the Potomac*. Fairfax, Va.: Fairfax County Office of Comprehensive Planning.

Stoddart, James. 1718. *A ground platt of the city and port of Annapolis*. Maryland State Archives, Special Collections 1427-1-3.

Tallichet, Marjorie D., compiler. 1986. *Alexandria city directory 1791*. Bowie, Md.: Heritage.

Thompson's. 1852. *Thompson's Mercantile and Professional Directory (1851–1852)*. CD-ROM by History Broker, Alexandria Library Special Collections.

Troupe, Charles G. 1980. *Archaeological excavations on Colchester, Virginia, lot 39 (44FX119)*. Master's thesis, University of Idaho. Copy on file at the Alexandria Library Special Collections.

Tunis, Edwin. 1972. *Colonial craftsmen and the beginning of American industry*. New York: World Publishing.

Veloz, Nicholas F., compiler. 1978. *Butcher, baker, candlestick maker, the 1810 census and personal property tax rolls for Alexandria, Virginia*. Unpublished manuscript, Barret Library, Alexandria, Va.

Virginian [Janney, Samuel M.]. 1844. The benefits of free labor. *Alexandria Gazette*, December 11.

Vlach, J. Michael. 1993. *Back of the big house: The architecture of plantation slavery*. Chapel Hill: University of North Carolina Press.

Walker, M. K., and T. Dennee. 1994. "*The receptacles were emptied of their contents*": *Archaeological testing of area II-B of the Carlyle property and excavation of Shuter's Hill Brewery site (44AX35), Alexandria, Virginia*. Report on file at the Alexandria Library Special Collections.

Wallerstein, Immanuel M. 1974. *The modern world-system: Capitalist agriculture and the origins of European world-economy in the sixteenth century.* New York: Academic.

———. 1976. *The modern world-system.* New York: Academic.

———. 1989. *The modern world-system, volume III: The second era of great expansion of the capitalist world-economy, 1730–1840.* New York: Academic.

Walsh, Lorena Seebach. 1977. *Charles County, Maryland, 1658–1705: A study of Chesapeake social and political structure.* Ph.D. diss., Michigan State University.

Walsh, Lorena S., Ann Smart Martin, and Joanne Bowen. 1997. *Provisioning early American towns.* Report prepared for the National Endowment for the Humanities.

Ward, Kimberly D. 2001. *The Henderson House.* The Weems-Botts Museum. At www.geocities.com/TheTropics/Equator/6490/hendersonhouse.html, accessed November 29, 2006.

Wardell, Patrick G., compiler. 1989. *Alexandria City and County, Virginia, deed book extracts volume 1, 1801–1818.* Bowie, Md.: Heritage.

Ware, Donna M. 1990. *Anne Arundel's legacy: The historic properties of Anne Arundel County.* Annapolis, Md.: Office of Planning and Zoning.

Weber, Max. 1992 [1930]. *The Protestant ethic and the spirit of capitalism.* Trans. Talcott Parsons. New York: Routledge.

Wilentz, Sean. 1984. *Chants democratic: New York City and the rise of the American working class, 1788–1850.* New York: Oxford University Press.

Wilk, Richard R. 1996. *Economies and cultures.* Boulder, Colo.: Westview.

Wilkie, Laurie A. 2000. *Creating freedom: Construction of African American identity at a Louisiana plantation.* Baton Rouge: Louisiana State University Press.

———. 2004. Considering the future of African American archaeology. *Historical Archaeology* 38 (1):109–23.

Wilkie, Laurie A., and Kevin M. Bartoy. 2000. A critical archaeology revisited. *Current Anthropology* 41:747–61.

Wockek, Marianne S. 1999. *Trade in strangers: The beginnings of mass migration to North America.* University Park: Pennsylvania State University Press.

Wolf, Eric. 1982. *Europe and the people without history*. Berkeley: University of California Press.

Wright, Henry T. 1959. *Notes on "Custom House" excavation, site number MS-3 (Market Square-3)*. Report on file at Historic Annapolis Foundation Archaeological Laboratory.

Yentsch, Anne Elizabeth. 1994. *A Chesapeake family and their slaves: A study in historical archaeology*. New York: Cambridge University Press.

Index

About the Author

The Chesapeake region always has something new and interesting to offer archaeologists. **Thomas W. Cuddy** grew up along the Potomac River, but first experienced historical archaeology along the James River excavating at Curles Neck Plantation and Jordan's Journey with the fieldschool from Virginia Commonwealth University, where he received a Bachelor of Science degree. He received M.A. and Ph.D. degrees from Columbia University, based on three seasons of excavation at the Maya site of Chau Hiix, Belize. While finishing his degree he was scientific assistant at the American Museum of Natural History. He went on to conduct a two-year post doctoral fellowship at the Smithsonian Institution researching museum collections from northeast Honduras, then became the curator of archaeology for the Historic Annapolis Foundation. He has taught courses on historical archaeology as well as the rise of civilizations, and his research interests explore topics of economic interaction, cultural identity, and the development of sociopolitical complexity in prehistoric and historic settings. He has worked on archaeological projects across the tidewater Chesapeake region, from the peaceful Wye Island on Maryland's eastern shore to downtown Washington, D.C. He lives with his family in Alexandria.